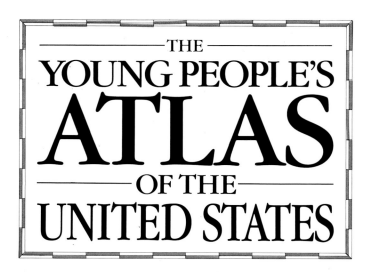

THE
YOUNG PEOPLE'S
ATLAS
OF THE
UNITED STATES

Design
Kelly Flynn

Picture Research
Jane Duff

Editor
Kate Phelps

Editorial Assistant
Claire Berridge

Typesetting
Bob Gordon Design

Maps
Malcolm Porter
Swanston Graphics (U.S.A. map)

Illustrations
David Wright (state symbols)
Trevor Lawrence (flags)

KINGFISHER BOOKS
Grisewood & Dempsey Inc.
95 Madison Avenue
New York, New York 10016

First edition 1992

10 9 8 7 6 5 4 3 2

Library of Congress Cataloging-in-Publication Data
The young people's atlas of the United States/James Harrison:
consultant, Professor Jack Zevin
p. cm
Summary: An atlas of the United States, containing color maps and
photographs covering each state's major cities, landscape, industry,
agriculture, and history.

1. United States — Maps. [1. United States — Maps.] I. Title.
II. Title: Atlas of the United States.
G1200. H39 1992 <G & M>
912.73 — dc20   92-53116 CIP MAP AC

ISBN 1-85697-804-4

Printed in Spain

THE
YOUNG PEOPLE'S
ATLAS
OF THE
UNITED STATES

James Harrison
Eleanor Van Zandt
Consultant: Professor Jack Zevin

Kingfisher Books

NEW YORK

CONTENTS

FEATURES OF THIS BOOK

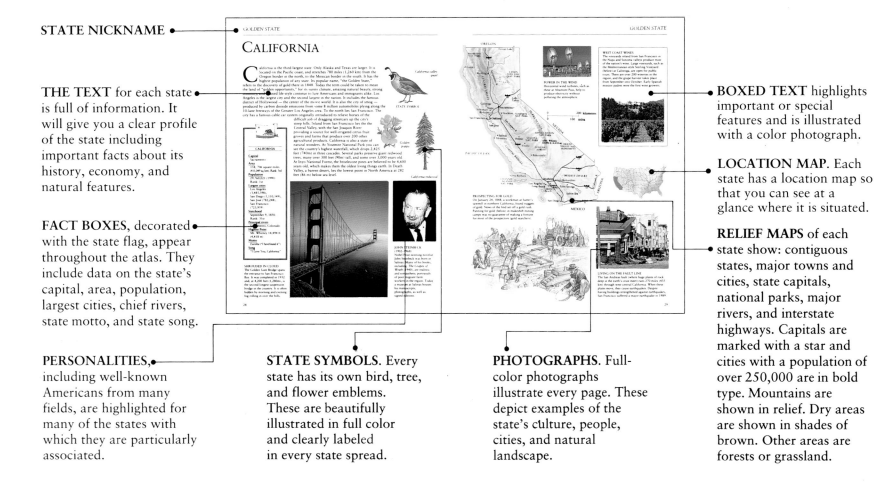

STATE NICKNAME

THE TEXT for each state is full of information. It will give you a clear profile of the state including important facts about its history, economy, and natural features.

FACT BOXES, decorated with the state flag, appear throughout the atlas. They include data on the state's capital, area, population, largest cities, chief rivers, state motto, and state song.

PERSONALITIES, including well-known Americans from many fields, are highlighted for many of the states with which they are particularly associated.

STATE SYMBOLS. Every state has its own bird, tree, and flower emblems. These are beautifully illustrated in full color and clearly labeled in every state spread.

PHOTOGRAPHS. Full-color photographs illustrate every page. These depict examples of the state's culture, people, cities, and natural landscape.

BOXED TEXT highlights important or special features and is illustrated with a color photograph.

LOCATION MAP. Each state has a location map so that you can see at a glance where it is situated.

RELIEF MAPS of each state show: contiguous states, major towns and cities, state capitals, national parks, major rivers, and interstate highways. Capitals are marked with a star and cities with a population of over 250,000 are in bold type. Mountains are shown in relief. Dry areas are shown in shades of brown. Other areas are forests or grassland.

INTRODUCTION

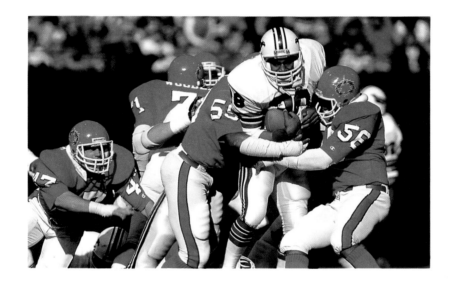

THE YOUNG PEOPLE'S ATLAS OF THE UNITED STATES invites you to take a tour of a country that is one of the world's largest, wealthiest, and most geographically exciting areas. Explore the variety of landscapes and peoples that live in the United States, and discover some of its natural beauties and cultural symbols. Find out how the ecology of a state and a region influences its history, character, products, and pastimes.

Don't think of this Atlas as merely a collection of maps, but as a guide to those features and people who have shaped the land and used its resources. Decide how the rivers and mountains, plains and valleys, deserts and forests of the United States have sometimes aided, and other times slowed, economic and political development.

Collect information about climate and weather, geology and geography, plants and animals, cities and towns, industries and agriculture for each state, region, and the nation as a whole. Pick out a favorite state and learn more about it. Choose a place you would most like to visit. Imagine yourself discovering new territory . . . but remember that someone may have been there before you!

Travel through each state of the Union. Put groups of states together into regions. Then view the states and regions as a single, connected whole . . . one nation with a history that might be described as always changing. Change and movement have characterized the United States from the time of its original peoples, the native American Indian groups, through exploration by European explorers and a revolutionary birth and Civil War ordeal, to its present status as a superpower in world affairs.

Change has also brought about many problems, and you will learn about some of the important ones in this Atlas. The wonders of nature that the United States contains have often been wisely set aside in national parks and forests. But the progress of technology and industry that have provided a high standard of living have also sometimes damaged the environment through pollution and the destruction of habitats. The many immigrants and pioneers who have contributed to the rich culture of the United States have also sometimes clashed with those who went before them, or with each other. Native Americans, African Americans, those of different religions or ethnic groups have often had to struggle to take advantage of the society's wealth and power.

However, problems and all, the story of the fifty states tells about a land of dramatic scenery and plentiful resources. In the cities and towns, suburbs and farms of the United States live millions of people descended from immigrants who came from other lands: Africa, Asia, Europe, and Latin America. All of these form a people who have bonded with their new land, and who share its advantages and its problems.

Often, the face of the earth has been altered to serve human needs through the building of dams, canals, harbors, bridges, and monuments. At other times, areas have been set aside for their beauty, to preserve unique plant and animal life, or to provide for human recreation. Are there any natural places described in this Atlas that you would especially like to see? Are there any human creations or works that you think are amazing? Are there any individuals or peoples that you find particularly interesting? Take us up on our invitation to use this Atlas as a way of exploring the great and fascinating country that is the United States of America.

Professor Jack Zevin
Queens College, City University of New York

THE UNITED STATES

The United States of America is located (apart from Hawaii) on the continent of North America, which it shares with Canada, Mexico, and the countries of Central America. Often, however, the name "North America" is applied just to Canada and the United States, to distinguish them from their Spanish-speaking neighbors to the south. The name "America" is also commonly used to mean the United States.

The United States includes the 50 states plus the District of Columbia, or Washington, the capital, which is a self-governing city. You will sometimes find the terms "the nation" or "the Union" used to mean the United States (although during the Civil War the "Union" meant the North, as opposed to the Confederacy of southern states).

To refer to the 48 states that touch each other (that is, excluding Hawaii and Alaska) the term "continental United States" is normally used. You will also sometimes find these states called the "contiguous states." The continental United States is bordered on the north by Canada, which is larger in size by 230,230 square miles (596,296 sq. km); on the south by Mexico and the Gulf of Mexico; on the east by the Atlantic Ocean; and on the west by the Pacific. The United States has a number of possessions, including the Commonwealth of Puerto Rico and various Pacific islands.

◁ A traditional sledge crosses the frozen tundra of the northernmost state, Alaska. The state has a vast wealth of natural resources.

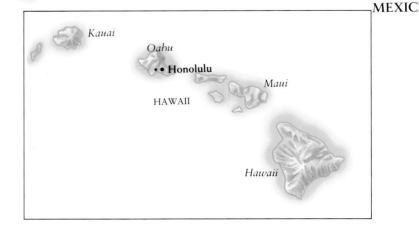

◁ The volcanic islands of Hawaii form the farthest western extent of the United States.

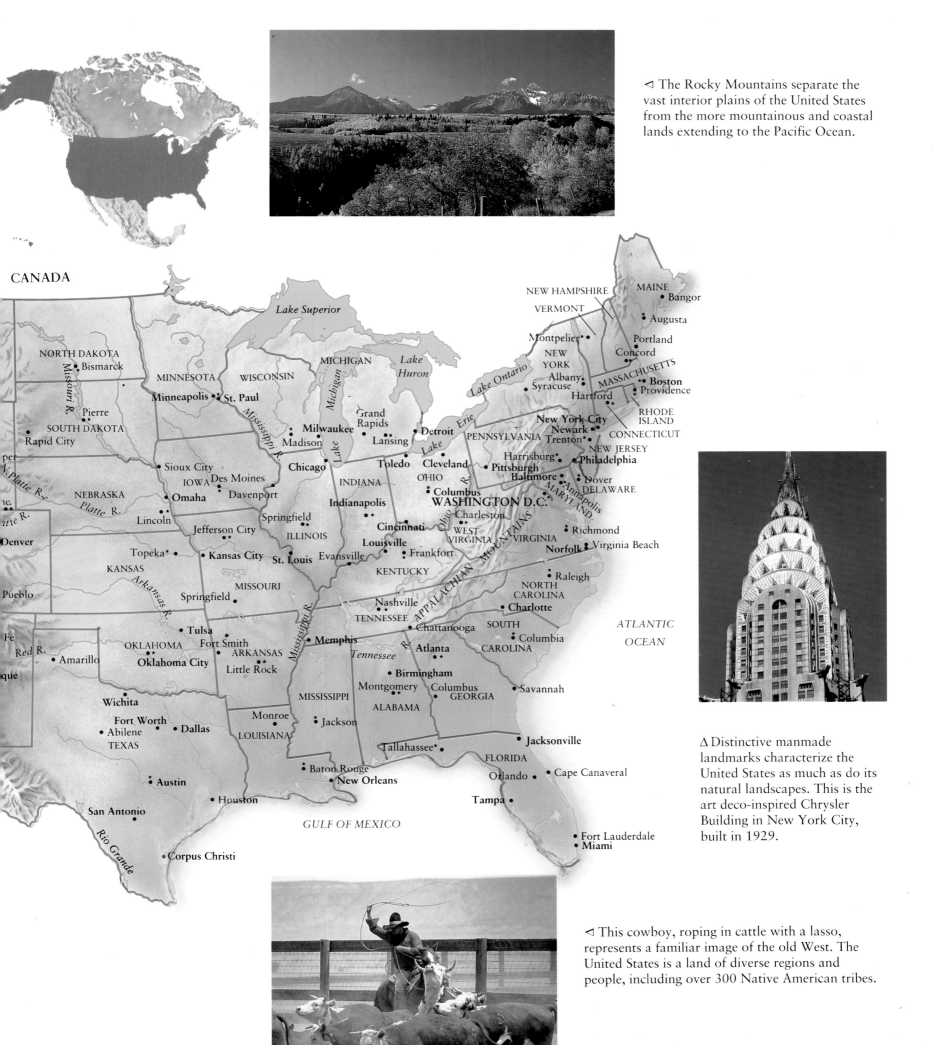

◁ The Rocky Mountains separate the vast interior plains of the United States from the more mountainous and coastal lands extending to the Pacific Ocean.

CANADA

Lake Superior

NORTH DAKOTA
• Bismarck

MICHIGAN
Lake Huron

NEW HAMPSHIRE
MAINE
• Bangor

VERMONT
• Augusta

Portland
Montpelier •
Concord

MINNESOTA
WISCONSIN

Pierre
• Minneapolis • St. Paul

SOUTH DAKOTA
Rapid City

Missouri R.

Mississippi R.

NEW YORK
Albany •
MASSACHUSETTS
Syracuse
• Boston
Hartford • Providence

Milwaukee
Grand Rapids
Madison Lansing
Detroit
Lake Erie

Lake Michigan

Lake Ontario

RHODE ISLAND
CONNECTICUT

Sioux City
Chicago
Toledo Cleveland
PENNSYLVANIA
New York City
Newark •
Trenton •
NEW JERSEY

IOWA Des Moines
INDIANA
Harrisburg •
Philadelphia
Pittsburgh
Baltimore
Dover
DELAWARE

NEBRASKA
Omaha
Davenport
OHIO
Columbus
MARYLAND
Annapolis

Platte R.
Springfield
Indianapolis
WASHINGTON D.C.

N. Platte R.
Lincoln
Jefferson City
ILLINOIS
Cincinnati
Charleston
WEST VIRGINIA
VIRGINIA
Richmond

Denver
Topeka •
Kansas City
St. Louis
Louisville
Frankfort
Norfolk • Virginia Beach

Pueblo
KANSAS
Arkansas R.
MISSOURI
Evansville
KENTUCKY

Raleigh
Springfield
NORTH CAROLINA

Fe
OKLAHOMA
Tulsa
Nashville
Chattanooga
Charlotte

Red R.
Fort Smith
TENNESSEE
APPALACHIAN MOUNTAINS
SOUTH
Columbia
CAROLINA

ATLANTIC OCEAN

Amarillo
Oklahoma City
ARKANSAS
Little Rock
Memphis
Tennessee R.
Atlanta

que
Mississippi R.
Birmingham
Montgomery
Columbus
GEORGIA
Savannah

Wichita
MISSISSIPPI
ALABAMA

Fort Worth
Monroe
Jackson

Abilene • Dallas
LOUISIANA
Jacksonville

TEXAS
Tallahassee •
FLORIDA

Austin
Baton Rouge
New Orleans
Orlando •
Cape Canaveral

Houston
Tampa •

San Antonio

Rio Grande

GULF OF MEXICO

Fort Lauderdale
Miami

Corpus Christi

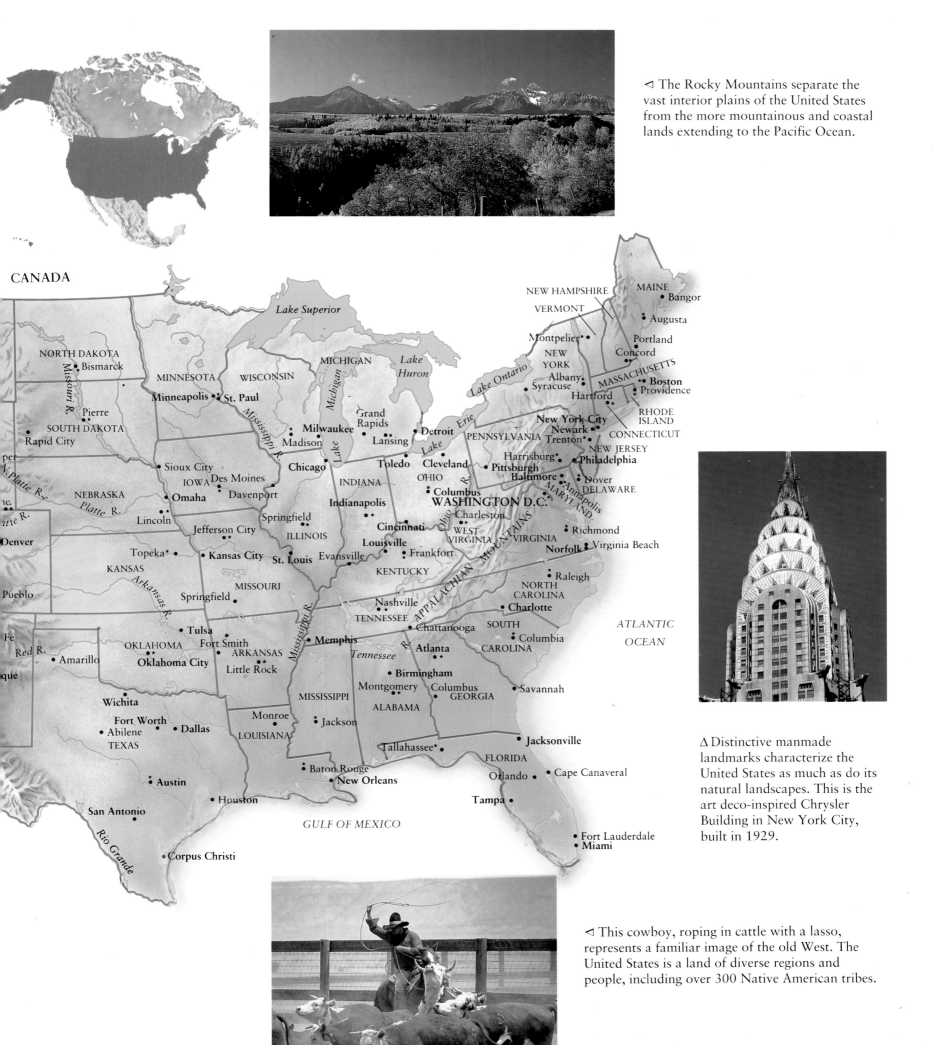

△ Distinctive manmade landmarks characterize the United States as much as do its natural landscapes. This is the art deco-inspired Chrysler Building in New York City, built in 1929.

◁ This cowboy, roping in cattle with a lasso, represents a familiar image of the old West. The United States is a land of diverse regions and people, including over 300 Native American tribes.

THE NORTHEASTERN STATES

The Northeastern region of the United States includes the Middle Atlantic states of New York, New Jersey, and Pennsylvania, and the six New England states: Maine, Massachusetts, New Hampshire, Vermont, Rhode Island, and Connecticut. The dominant physical feature of the Northeast is the Appalachian Mountains — a 1,600-mile (2,575-km) long crescent of mountains stretching from the St. Lawrence Valley in Canada down to northern Alabama. They comprise many smaller ranges, including the Green Mountains of Vermont, the White Mountains of New Hampshire, the Alleghenies of Pennsylvania, and the Adirondacks and Catskills of New York. The Northeast has a varied coastline, ranging from the sandy beaches of New Jersey to the rocky shores of Maine.

The name "New England" was given to this extreme northeast area by Captain John Smith, who explored its coast in 1614. In some ways the land does resemble England, and because the first colonists here were nearly all English, there are also many English place-names, such as Plymouth and Manchester.

A little farther south, other nations colonized this region — the Dutch in what is now New York and the Germans and Swedes in Pennsylvania — along with many English as well. In addition to farming, these northeastern settlers established industries, such as fishing, whaling, and shipbuilding. They founded many towns, some of which now rank among the nation's most important cities, such as Boston, Philadelphia, and New York. There are many historic sites in the Northeast, particularly from the Colonial and Revolutionary War periods.

△ There are many small farms on the fertile plains of the Northeast, although agriculture is less important in the region than industry or commerce.

◁ Many of the first New England settlers were Puritans, who practiced a simple way of life. Today, some religious sects pursue time-honored lifestyles, such as this farmer with his plow and horses.

▷ White painted, clapboard churches and houses dot the gently rolling, tree-lined Vermont landscape, which bursts into red and gold in the fall.

◁ Religious freedom was the chief driving force for the first immigrants to the Northeast. Several of the early colonies were governed by religious leaders, and churches such as this were the focal point of the community.

△ The Northeast is steeped in the heritage of the Revolutionary War. It was here that the fighting began between American colonists and British troops. Many important events of the war are commemorated in this region.

◁ New York is the largest city in the United States and the country's commercial and cultural "nerve center." It has a thriving port, the busiest in the region, and boasts the second-tallest building in the United States — the World Trade Center.

9

THE SOUTHERN STATES

The South is a large region of great geographical variety. Parts of it are mountainous, crossed by the lower end of the Appalachian Mountains, including the Blue Ridge and Great Smoky ranges. Although relatively low, compared to the Rockies, for example, these mountains were, in earlier times, a barrier against westward migration.

The humid, subtropical southern lowlands contain many swamps, such as the Dismal Swamp of Virginia and North Carolina, the Louisiana bayous, and the Florida Everglades. Some of these marshy areas, once dangerous places, teeming with disease-bearing mosquitoes, are now important wildlife reserves.

The warm climate and fertile soil of the southern plateaus are ideal for the cultivation of many crops, notably tobacco and cotton. It was the mainly cotton-based economy of the South, dominated by large plantations and run by slave labor, that led to the Civil War in 1861. Eleven Southern states, insisting on their right to maintain slavery against growing opposition from the North, seceded from the Union and formed the Confederate States of America. Only after four years of bitter fighting was the Union restored and slavery finally abolished. The South bears many marks of that struggle, in the form of memorials, statues, cemeteries, and battlefields.

But although the South is a strongly tradition-conscious region, it is an increasingly progressive one, with many high-tech industries located there. The nation's capital, Washington, D.C. (District of Columbia), is also located in the South, between Maryland and Virginia.

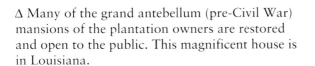

△ Many of the grand antebellum (pre-Civil War) mansions of the plantation owners are restored and open to the public. This magnificent house is in Louisiana.

◁ Bald cypress trees draped in Spanish moss line many rivers, swamps, and bayous in the South. The subtropical flora and fauna give this region a distinctive character, unlike that of any other part of the United States.

Δ The South boasts the world famous Walt Disney World which includes the Epcot Center. It is situated in Florida.

DISTRICT OF COLUMBIA

The District of Columbia is the seat of government of the United States. It covers the same area as the city of Washington, D.C. The Constitution provided that an area of land be set aside for the new nation's capital and it was authorized by Congress in 1790. George Washington named his choice of a location for the city in 1791. He hired a French architect, Pierre Charles L'Enfant, to design the city. In 1800, the federal government moved the capital from Philadelphia. The District of Columbia was originally made up of small portions of Maryland and Virginia but the Virginia land was returned to that state in 1846. During the Civil War, Confederate territory began just over the Potomac River, in Virginia.

Because Washington is a district, not a state, its residents used to have fewer rights than other U.S. citizens. For example, until 1961, they did not have the right to vote in presidential elections. Many famous historic buildings are situated in the city. The Jefferson Memorial, Washington Monument, and Lincoln Memorial pay tribute to three of America's greatest presidents. Today Washington, D.C. is probably the most important center of government in the world.

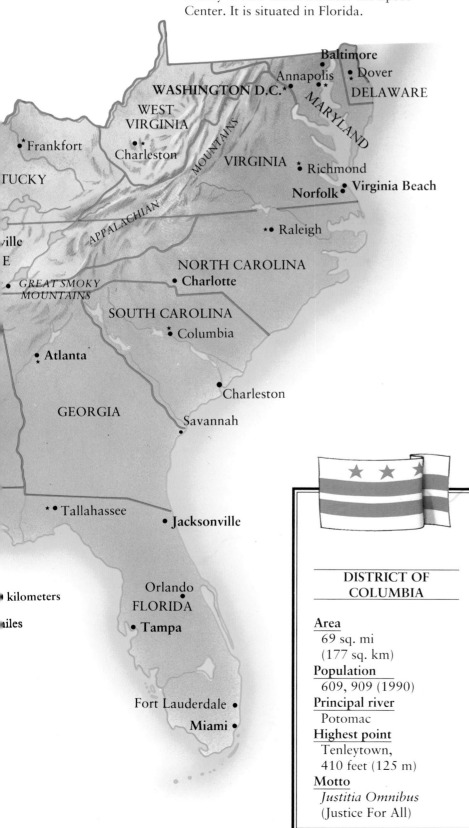

DISTRICT OF COLUMBIA

Area
69 sq. mi
(177 sq. km)
Population
609, 909 (1990)
Principal river
Potomac
Highest point
Tenleytown,
410 feet (125 m)
Motto
Justitia Omnibus
(Justice For All)

HISTORIC CITY
The centerpiece of the nation's capital, Washington, D.C., is its impressive Capitol building on Capitol Hill. The building (above) has undergone many changes since it was first designed by William Thornton. The federal government is conducted in its House of Representatives and Senate. The Library of Congress is also in Washington. The President of the United States lives in his official residence, the White House, at 1600 Pennsylvania Avenue. Every president except Washington has lived there. Within the Lincoln Memorial, the statue of a seated President Lincoln (right) faces the Washington Monument — a 555-foot (169-m) high obelisk, which can be ascended by elevator. One of the newest monuments is dedicated to the men and women who died in the Vietnam War.

THE MIDWESTERN STATES

The Midwest occupies the center of the United States. It adjoins all the other regions, as well as Canada. The land was formed mainly by glaciers retreating after an Ice Age millions of years ago. These huge masses of ice flattened much of the terrain in the south and left deposits of rich soil. Farming predominates in the region, and the Midwest has long been the "breadbasket" of the United States. It produces most of the country's grain — spring wheat in the north, winter wheat and corn in the center and south. Soybeans are an important crop, especially in Iowa. Only the Badlands and the Black Hills of South Dakota are unsuitable for crops.

The Midwest is also rich in minerals, and iron and steel industries are located here in towns such as Gary, Indiana, and Detroit, Michigan. Chicago is the largest city in the Midwest. It also boasts the nation's, and the world's, tallest building, the Sears Tower. The city stands on the shores of Lake Michigan, one of the five Great Lakes, which form the region's northeastern border.

The Great Lakes alone contain 99 percent of all the fresh water in the country. Several states are dotted with thousands of lesser lakes — Michigan, Minnesota, and Wisconsin have more than 10,000 apiece. The Mississippi–Missouri river system helps to shape the geography and economy of the region. Over 12 percent of the total area of North America is drained by the Mississippi and its tributaries. The Midwest accounts for some 20 percent of the total land area, and a quarter of the nation's population. Much of the Midwest was bought from France in 1803 by the U.S. government as part of the Louisiana Purchase.

△ A barrier ridge known as the Wall rises from the prairie in the Badlands National Park, South Dakota. Pioneers feared these fluted escarpments and gave the area the name Badlands. Herds of bison and bighorn sheep now roam the land.

◁ Much of the Midwest is vast, flat prairie which has been cultivated to produce a large portion of the nation's wheat and other staple crops. These combine harvesters are in Kansas, the leading wheat-growing state.

◁◁ The Black Hills of South Dakota include Mt. Rushmore, which is carved with the massive likenesses of four presidents — Washington, Jefferson, Theodore Roosevelt, and Lincoln. The sculptor, Gutzon Borglum, was an American of Danish descent.

◁ Lakeshore Drive in Chicago runs along Lake Michigan. Chicago is the foremost commercial and cultural center of the Midwestern states.

△ A covered wooden bridge in Indiana. The roof protects passengers and the bridge itself. Many bridges were burned in accidents, but there are still some fine examples in the Midwest.

▷ President Abraham Lincoln spent his boyhood days in Indiana, and much of his adult life in Illinois. His early home is located south of Lincoln City, Indiana, at the Lincoln Boyhood National Monument.

THE SOUTHWESTERN STATES

The Southwestern states of Arizona, New Mexico, Texas, and Oklahoma tell another history of the United States, far removed from the better-known story of the Thirteen Colonies and their struggle for independence. From the 1500s to the mid-1800s this vast territory was dominated by Spaniards and then Mexicans. Spanish influence is still evident here, especially in the architecture and the place-names, such as Santa Fe ("Holy Faith"), the territory's first capital.

Here, too, the culture of Native Americans remains visible. Ancient tribes such as the Anasazi, Zuñi, and Hopi flourished as long as 15,000 years ago. They hunted bison and mammoths, and later probably developed the first agriculture on the continent, as well as crafts such as basket weaving and pottery. When the Spanish arrived, they found settled communities, whose village culture they called simply *Pueblo* ("town").

The Southwest is a region of vast open plains, mountains, and desert. Its most renowned feature is the Grand Canyon, in Arizona, a 277-mile (450-km) -long gorge cut by the Colorado River. With a depth in places of one mile (1.6 km), the canyon reveals, in its many layers of beautifully colored rock, the development of the continent over hundreds of millions of years.

Oklahoma was the earliest part of the Southwest to be acquired by the United States, as part of the Louisiana Purchase of 1803. The state of Texas joined the Union in 1845, and most of the remaining southwest territory was acquired as a result of the Mexican War (1846–1848).

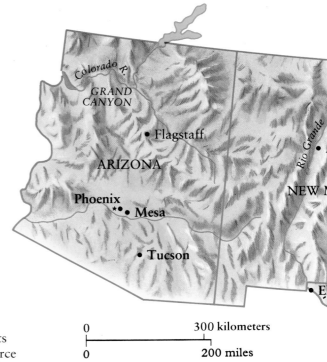

◁ The weaving of traditional blankets provides Navajos with a valuable source of income. Navajos are the largest tribe of Native Americans, with some 160,000 in the Southwest.

▷ Spectacular sandstone monoliths rise up in Arizona's Monument Valley. At sunset they cast long shadows over the great expanse of plateau.

◁ The White Sands National Monument in New Mexico contains great deposits of wind-blown gypsum sand. In strong light, the sands look like a giant snowfield.

◁ The Southwest is the largest oil-producing region, with Texas ranked as the first oil-producing state, Oklahoma fifth, and New Mexico seventh. Much of the oil is extracted from the Gulf of Mexico.

Δ Cattle herding is still done by cowboys on horseback, as it was in the mid-1800s, on many of the vast ranches of the Southwest.

▷ This sculpture by the famous Spanish artist, Joan Miró, is located in Houston, Texas, the country's fourth-largest city. Houston is well known for its distinctive examples of modern architecture, such as these towering skyscrapers.

THE ROCKY MOUNTAIN STATES

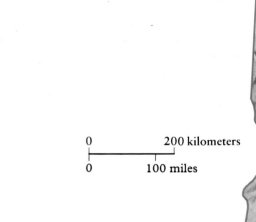

As their name suggests, the Rocky Mountain states of Colorado, Utah, Wyoming, Montana, Nevada, and Idaho are crossed by this great mountain range — the greatest in North America. The Rockies extend from north to south through the west-central United States. Running along the crest of the mountains is the Continental Divide. Rain falling east of this line forms rivulets and then larger streams and rivers that eventually drain into the Gulf of Mexico or the Great Lakes and on into the Atlantic. Rain falling to the west of it eventually reaches the Pacific.

The Rockies contain several national parks. The best known of these, located mainly in Wyoming, is Yellowstone National Park, which is famous for its many geysers and abundant wildlife. Elk, moose, wolves, and even grizzly bears inhabit this natural wonderland. Grand Teton Park, also in Wyoming, boasts some of the most spectacular peaks in the Rockies, the highest being Grand Teton itself, at 13,770 feet (4,200 m).

This region is also rich in minerals — oil, natural gas, copper, gold, silver, lead, zinc, and molybdenum. Farming, too, is important, with thousands of acres devoted to sheep and cattle raising and to crops such as wheat and potatoes.

The largest city of the Rocky Mountain region is Denver, Colorado, which is also one of the highest cities in the United States, with an elevation of exactly one mile (1.6 km). Earlier Native American inhabitants of Colorado farmed the high mesas and built their homes in the sandstone cliffs. These amazing cliff dwellings can still be seen today in Mesa Verde National Park.

0		200 kilometers
0		100 miles

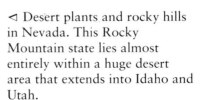

◁ Desert plants and rocky hills in Nevada. This Rocky Mountain state lies almost entirely within a huge desert area that extends into Idaho and Utah.

▷ This snowy scene in Idaho is typical of the Rocky Mountain states in winter. A herd of cattle braves the freezing conditions.

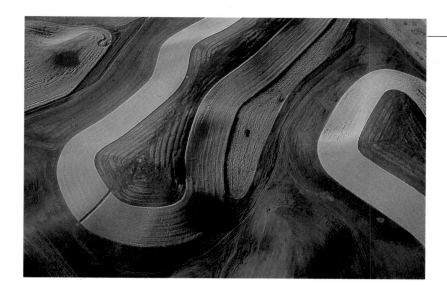

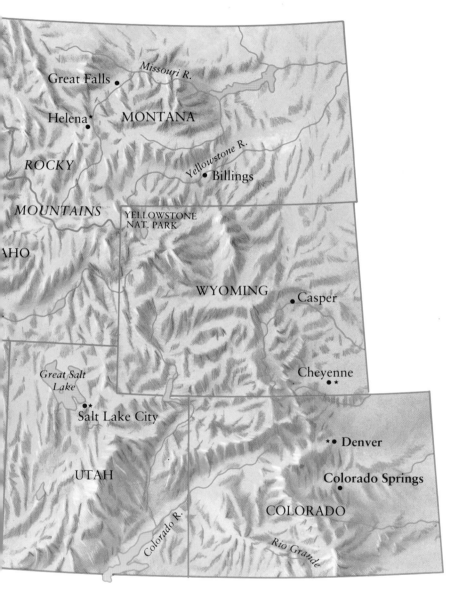

◁ △ An aerial view of farmland contours in Idaho. Rocky Mountain crops include the famous Idaho potato; hay, wheat, barley, oats, and fruit are also grown in the region.

△ As its name implies, Old Faithful geyser, in Yellowstone National Park, keeps on gushing regularly without fail. It does so at least every half-hour, when it spews out 5-7,000 gallons (19-27,000 liters) of hot water.

△ With so many great rivers flowing through the Rocky Mountains, water sports, especially white-water rafting, draw thousands of vacationers to these states each year.

◁ Breath-taking mountain scenery is a distinctive feature of this region. There are numerous lakes, waterfalls, hot springs, and glaciers.

THE PACIFIC COAST STATES

The Pacific Coast states are the nation's last western frontier. They embrace a vast area of the earth's surface — from the three adjoining states of California, Oregon, and Washington, to Alaska in the far northwest and Hawaii, halfway across the Pacific Ocean. Anchorage, on Alaska's south coast, lies 1,500 miles (2,415 km) north of Seattle, in Washington, and Honolulu is 2,500 miles (4,025 km) from Los Angeles. By contrast, the westernmost point of Alaska is only 50 miles (80 km) from Siberia, across the Bering Strait.

Their enormous geographical spread gives the Pacific Coast states the greatest variety of any region, ranging from the frozen tundra of Alaska to the lush, green volcanic terrain of Hawaii. The mountains, valleys, and coastlines of the three contiguous states offer dramatic landscapes.

In their different ways, the Pacific states are among the richest in natural resources, particularly oil and timber. The vast forests of Oregon and Washington supply more of the nation's timber than any other region, and California's fertile valleys produce fruit and vegetables in abundance.

The physical diversity of the Pacific states is matched by their ethnic diversity. As well as Inuit (Eskimos), and native Hawaiians, there are many Asian, white, black, and Hispanic settlers.

◁ The Space Needle dominates the Seattle skyline on Puget Sound. This, the largest city in Washington, is surrounded by snowcapped mountains of the Cascade Range.

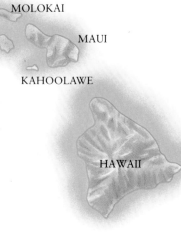

△ ▷ A large walrus colony rests on the shores of the Bering Sea, at the westernmost tip of Alaska.

◁ Hawaii is not all volcanic craters, tropical forests, and sandy beaches. Inland are important farming areas. These fields either side of the river are growing taro, an edible root vegetable.

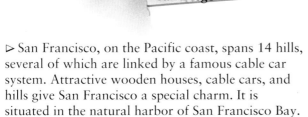

△ Mountains and rocks line the shore at Cannon Beach in Oregon. The state's coastline extends 296 miles (476 km) along the Pacific Ocean.

◁ Market gardening is an important industry in Washington, Oregon, and California. Apples, citrus fruits, and flowers thrive here. The region also produces most of North America's wine.

▷ San Francisco, on the Pacific coast, spans 14 hills, several of which are linked by a famous cable car system. Attractive wooden houses, cable cars, and hills give San Francisco a special charm. It is situated in the natural harbor of San Francisco Bay.

ALABAMA

Located in the heart of the Deep South, Alabama is a state with a rich conflict-filled history. It is a history of wealthy cotton plantations (with the slavery they were based on), bloody civil war, and later social and political change. It was in Montgomery, the state capital, that the Confederate States of America were established on February 4, 1861. The First White House of the Confederacy is located in the city. It was also in Alabama that many of the important events in the civil rights campaigns of the 1950s and 1960s took place.

Alabama has a short strip of coastline on the Gulf of Mexico, dominated by the city of Mobile, at the mouth of the Mobile River. The state's mild climate and rich soil make it an important farming state, growing the traditional southern crops of peanuts, cotton, and pecans. Alabama is also a large lumber producer, and pulp and paper processing are important sources of income. But the state has also taken on 20th-century industries, including electronics and the space industry. Birmingham is the South's leading steel center. Alabama has large reserves of the three most important raw materials used in steel making — coal, limestone, and iron ore. Most of Alabama's farms are located in the fertile, low-lying southern areas. The north is hilly and forested, with many rivers and lakes. Many of the state's rivers have been harnessed to provide power via hydroelectric power stations and dams.

Alabama was occupied by the French and Spanish before the entire region was ceded to England by the French at the end of the French and Indian War in 1763. However, Alabama continued to attract French settlers. The area later became a flourishing cotton-producing center, and some of its fine antebellum houses can still be visited. The Mobile Bay area, including the Gulf Coast State Park, is Alabama's leading tourist area. Its attractions include Bienville Square in Mobile itself, and the Bellingrath Gardens, 20 miles (32 km) south of the town. Another of the state's attractions that can be visited is Arlington Home and Gardens in Birmingham. This Greek revival house is the oldest structure in the city and the only mansion to survive the Civil War.

STATE SYMBOLS

Yellowhammer

Southern pine

Camellia

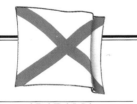

ALABAMA

Capital
Montgomery
Area
51,705 sq. mi
(133,916 sq. km)
Population
4,040,587 (1990)
Largest cities
Birmingham (265,968),
Mobile (196,278),
Montgomery (187,106)
Statehood
December 14, 1819
Rank: 22nd
Principal rivers
Tombigbee, Alabama,
Tennessee
Highest point
Cheaha,
2,407 feet (734 m)
Motto
*Audemus Jura Nostra
Defendere* (We Dare
Defend Our Rights)
Song
"Alabama"

HELEN KELLER
Writer and scholar, Helen Keller, was born in Alabama in 1880. Deaf, blind and almost without speech from the age of two, Keller (far left) was taught to read, write, and speak by Anne Sullivan (left). Keller "listened" by putting her fingers on the speaker's nose, lips, and throat, and read using braille — a special alphabet for the blind.

TUSKEGEE UNIVERSITY
White Hall, at Tuskegee University, the nation's oldest seat of learning for black Americans. The school was founded by former slave Booker T. Washington in 1881. He served as principal and instructor for 33 years. George Washington Carver, the famous scientific farmer, studied and taught at the college.

ALABAMA'S SPACE CENTER

The Space and Rocket Center is in Huntsville, in north-central Alabama, and is run by NASA (the National Aeronautics and Space Administration). It is said to be the largest space museum in the world. Visitors can become "astronauts" for a day, experience the sensation of weightlessness on a zero-gravity machine, and guide a spacecraft by computer. Huntsville is also the location of the U. S. Army's Redstone Arsenal and the George C. Marshall Space Flight Center. It was at Huntsville that the booster rockets which carried the Apollo Spacecraft to the moon in 1969 were made.

BROWN BOMBER

Joe Louis was one of America's greatest boxers. He was born in Alabama in 1914. In the late 1930s he won the world heavyweight title. Over 12 years he successfully defended his title 25 times — 20 of these ended in knockouts. Louis, nicknamed the Brown Bomber, retired undefeated, the longest-reigning world heavyweight champion in history. He died in 1981.

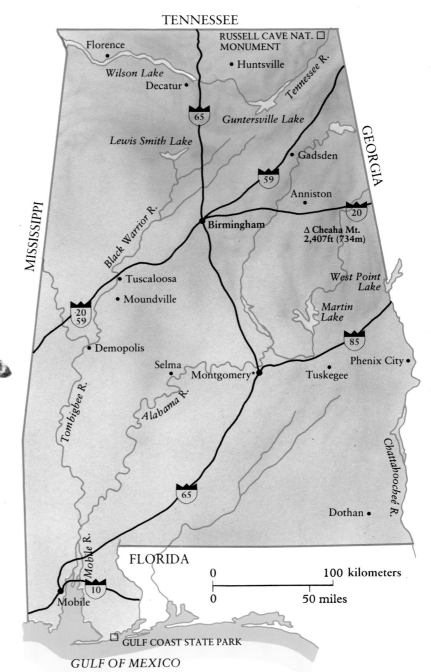

RACCOON

Raccoons live in woods near water. They are found in Alabama and all over the United States. These animals are nighttime hunters and scavengers. They have been hunted for their furs — first by Native Americans and later by white settlers, who used the furs as early currency.

COTTON WAS KING

Alabama's wealth came originally from cotton until the 1930s, when insect damage from the boll weevil pest, and competition from Texas and California, forced a decline in the cotton industry. Cotton is the soft white hairs, or fibers, that grow on the seeds of the cotton plant.

MOBILE'S SHIPS

Mobile, on the Gulf of Mexico, is the site of the Battleship *U.S.S. Alabama* Memorial Park. The battleship saw action in World War II and was one of the largest ever built. Next to it is the submarine *Drum*. Both may be boarded by visitors. Alabama's State Docks, at Mobile, have made the city an important ocean port. South of the city are beautiful sandy beaches for vacationers. Also in Mobile is Fort Condé–Charlotte, a re-creation of an 18th-century French fortress.

ALASKA

laska lives up to its unofficial nickname, "The Last Frontier." It is the most northerly state, a huge peninsula jutting out into the Arctic and Bering seas in the northwest corner of North America. It is completely separated from the continental United States by Canada. Alaska was bought by U.S. Secretary of State William H. Seward from the Russians in 1867. He paid $7.2 million — or about two cents per acre — but the deal was called "Seward's Folly" because the land seemed so desolate.

Almost a third of the state lies in the Arctic Circle, and much of the land is a vast wilderness of frozen tundra, glaciers, ice fields, lakes, spectacular mountains, and forests. It is also by far the largest state — double the land area of the second-largest state, Texas — but has the second-smallest state population. One-sixth of the people are native Alaskans — Inuits (Eskimos), Aleuts, and other Native American peoples. Aleuts, who gave the state its name, are related to Inuits but have their own language. Fishing is their main livelihood. Alaska's climate is quite varied. Some areas have harsh winters, but temperatures do not drop drastically on the Pacific coast because of the warming effect of the Japan Current. Winters are long, and the summer lasts just for June and July, when there are more daylight hours. This is the growing season for the inland valley farmlands, which produce barley, hay, and potatoes. The biggest industries by far are natural oil and gas, followed by tourism and fishing. Oil deposits were first discovered in the late 1950s. The 800-mile (1,300-km) Trans-Alaska Pipeline was built across the frozen wastes to the port of Valdez in the Alaskan Gulf. It was near here that the oil tanker *Exxon Valdez* spewed the largest oil spill in U.S. history in 1989. The oil slick spread for 45 miles (72 km).

STATE SYMBOLS

Willow ptarmigan

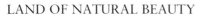

Forget-me-not

Sitka spruce

SIGNS IN THE SKY
Native American tribes, including Tlinglit and Haida, live in the milder southeast coastal regions. Totem poles are a visible part of their heritage.

LAND OF NATURAL BEAUTY
The mountains, fjords and glaciers, such as Mendenhall glacier (below), create a spectacular Arctic scenery that attracts thousands of tourists to Alaska. There are also many active volcanoes in the southeast and southwest of the state. Alaska boasts America's largest national park, Wrangell-St. Elias, covering 13,018 square miles (33,717 sq. km).

ALASKA
Capital
Juneau
Area
591,000 sq. mi
(1,530,571 sq. km)
Population
550,043 (1990)
Largest cities
Anchorage (226,338),
Fairbanks (30,843),
Juneau (26,751)
Statehood
January 3, 1959
Rank: 49th
Principal rivers
Yukon,
Kuskokwim
Highest point
Mt. McKinley 20,320 ft
(6,194 m); highest in
North America
Motto
North to the Future
Song
"Alaska's Flag"

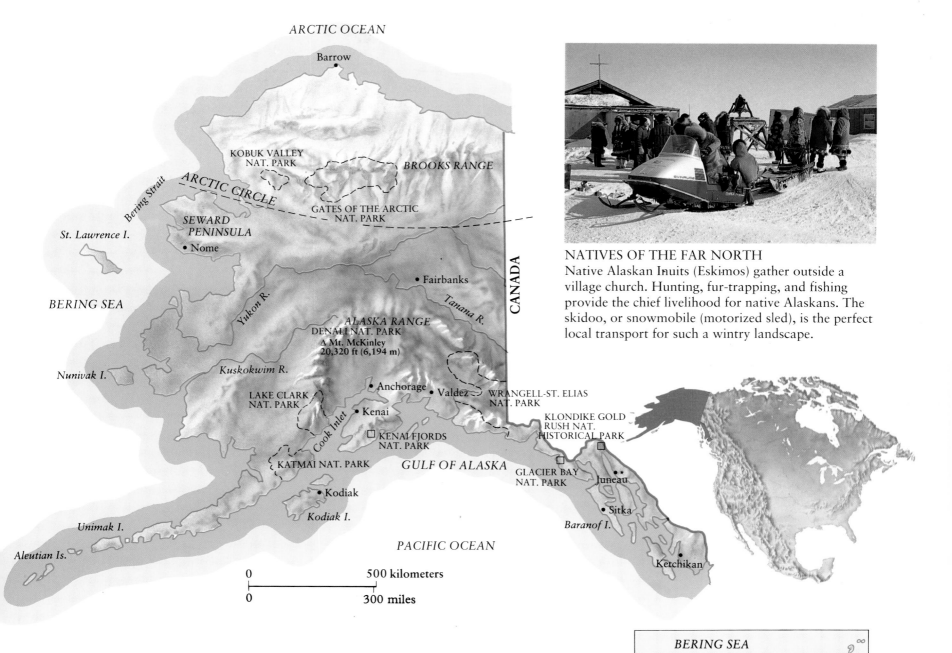

ARCTIC OCEAN

Barrow

KOBUK VALLEY
NAT. PARK

BROOKS RANGE

ARCTIC CIRCLE

GATES OF THE ARCTIC
NAT. PARK

Bering Strait

SEWARD
PENINSULA

St. Lawrence I.

• Nome

CANADA

• Fairbanks

BERING SEA

Yukon R.

Tanana R.

ALASKA RANGE
DENALI NAT. PARK
Δ Mt. McKinley
20,320 ft (6,194 m)

Nunivak I.

Kuskokwim R.

• Anchorage • Valdez

WRANGELL-ST. ELIAS
NAT. PARK

LAKE CLARK
NAT. PARK

Cook Inlet

• Kenai

KLONDIKE GOLD
RUSH NAT.
HISTORICAL PARK

KENAI FJORDS
NAT. PARK

KATMAI NAT. PARK

GULF OF ALASKA

GLACIER BAY
NAT. PARK

Juneau

• Kodiak

Kodiak I.

• Sitka

Baranof I.

Unimak I.

Aleutian Is.

PACIFIC OCEAN

Ketchikan

0   500 kilometers

0   300 miles

BERING SEA

Aleutian   Is.

PACIFIC OCEAN

NATIVES OF THE FAR NORTH
Native Alaskan Inuits (Eskimos) gather outside a village church. Hunting, fur-trapping, and fishing provide the chief livelihood for native Alaskans. The skidoo, or snowmobile (motorized sled), is the perfect local transport for such a wintry landscape.

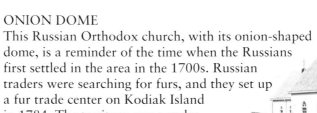

KING OF THE ICE
Swift on land and in the sea, polar bears hunt seals and fish for food. They grow to about 5 feet (1.5 m) in length and inhabit the frozen lands of Alaska and other Arctic regions.

COMMERCIAL CENTER
The business area and port of Anchorage — Alaska's largest city and business center — sits on the shores of Cook Inlet, which is part of the Gulf of Alaska. Huge icebergs regularly break off from glaciers along the gulf, and are carried out to sea by the Alaska Current. English explorer Captain Cook first visited the area in 1778. Oil is now the chief industry of the city.

ONION DOME
This Russian Orthodox church, with its onion-shaped dome, is a reminder of the time when the Russians first settled in the area in the 1700s. Russian traders were searching for furs, and they set up a fur trade center on Kodiak Island in 1784. The territory came under Russian control, and Alaska's first capital was founded at New Archangel (present-day Sitka) in 1804, where other Russian churches still stand. Sitka is a busy center of fishing and tourism on the west coast of Baranof Island.

ARIZONA

Arizona lies in the heart of the Southwest. It is an area of deserts, mountains, and plateaus, but is best known for being home to America's most famous natural feature — the Grand Canyon. At the canyon's western end lies Lake Mead (part of which is in Nevada and is the reservoir for Hoover Dam), which is one of the largest manmade lakes in the world. Other famous natural landscapes are the Painted Desert, a region of colorful wind-eroded hills, and the Petrified Forest, which has many fossilized trees that have turned to stone over millions of years, but have kept their tree-like appearance. The southern half of Arizona is part of the Sonoran (or Gila) Desert, which has many varieties of cactuses, such as the giant saguaro and organ pipe, found nowhere else in the world.

Irrigation has made this mainly barren land productive, with cotton and sorghum being among the chief crops. Air-conditioning helps people to endure the intense summer heat, and people have been coming to Arizona at a rate that makes it one of the fastest-growing states in the nation. Tourism is also a major industry, as are the manufacture of electronics and mining of molybdenum, gold, and silver. In the days of the Wild West, Tombstone, 30 miles (50 km) north of the Mexican border and the neighboring town of Bisbee were made rich by their silver mines.

The Spanish were the first Europeans to settle in the region, where they found Native American civilizations dating back to the 1100s. These Native Americans lived in *pueblos,* structured rather like modern apartment buildings, some four or five stories high. They irrigated and farmed the land. Tucson, the second-largest city, preserves much of its early Spanish flavor. The San Xavier del Bac Mission, near Tucson, was founded in 1692 by Spanish missionaries and is a historic landmark. The Spanish ruled it from the 1500s until 1821, when it became part of the newly independent Mexico. After the Mexican War of 1846 – 1848 the territory was given to the United States. In the 1860s, Arizona was also the site of fierce fighting when Apache and Navajo tribes fought white settlers and the U.S. Army. Today the state has the third-largest Native American population, and the largest amount of tribally-owned land.

STATE SYMBOLS

Cactus wren

Paloverde

Saguaro cactus

STATELY SAGUARO
Saguaro cactuses are the largest of the prickly plants, and can grow up to 40 feet (12 m) tall. The blossom, which is Arizona's state flower, appears for only a few days each spring.

AWESOME DESCENT
The Grand Canyon is a huge gorge of the Colorado River, etched across the northwestern corner of Arizona. It is 277 miles (450 km) long as the river runs, from 4 to 18 miles (6 to 30 km) wide, and a mile (1.6 km) deep.

DIGGING DEEP
This vast open-pit copper mine reflects Arizona's position as a leading copper producer. At one time, the state produced 12 percent of all the world's copper, and Arizona still accounts for over 75 percent of total U.S. output. The largest pit in the state is over 1,300 feet (400 m) deep. Copper is mined for its long-lasting, pliable, and non-rusting qualities, and it is used in the manufacture of wires and cables, as well as in boilers and radiators. However, such massive open-pit mining of the Earth's surface is a matter of concern to many environmentalists because of the damage it does to the landscape.

ARIZONA

Capital
Phoenix

Area
114,000 sq. mi
(295,240 sq. km)

Population
3,665,228 (1990)

Largest cities
Phoenix (983, 403),
Tucson (405, 390),
Mesa (288,091)

Statehood
February 14, 1912
Rank: 48th

Principal rivers
Colorado, Gila, Salt

Highest point
Humphreys Peak,
12,633 feet (3,853 m)

Motto
Ditat Deus
(God Enriches)

Song
"Arizona"

POISONOUS LIZARD
The Gila monster is aptly named for its looks, its poisonous bite, and its discovery in the Gila Desert. It lives in dry, scrubby areas, hiding in burrows by day and emerging at night to prey on small mammals, such as mice.

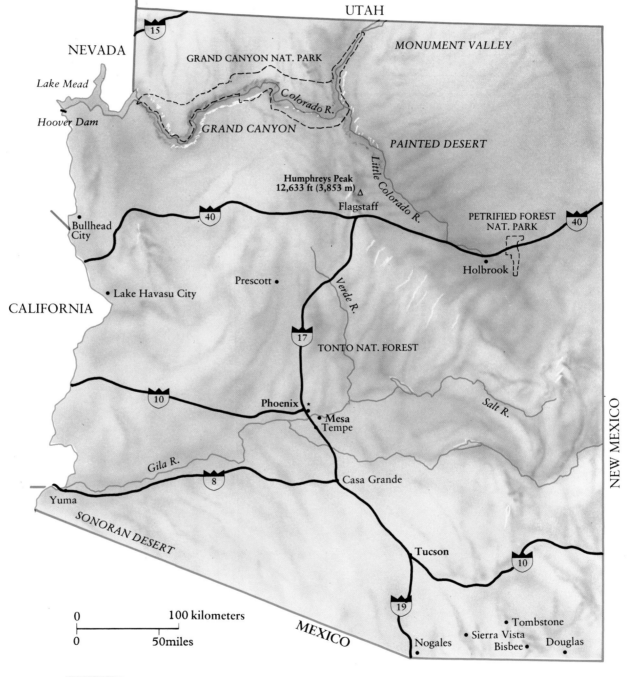

MONTEZUMA CASTLE
This 800-year-old cliff dwelling, in the center of Arizona, was built by Pueblo Indians. The 5-story, 20-room adobe brick structure was named "Montezuma castle" by early Spanish settlers who believed that it was built by Aztec refugees from Mexico — their emperor's name was Montezuma.

PHOENIX RISING
Named after the mythical bird that was burned and rose again from the ashes, Phoenix, with its many modern skyscrapers, rises out of the arid countryside. The city covers about 350 square miles (900 sq. km) and is located on the Salt River, in the south-central part of the state. It is the state capital and largest city, and the ninth-largest city in the United States. Phoenix is a center for electronic and computer industries, as well as for medicine. Most of Arizona's factories are located in and around the city.

ARKANSAS

Located in the south-central part of the United States, Arkansas is essentially a Southern state, but also has a western flavor. Its eastern and southern borders touch Mississippi, Tennessee, and Louisiana; on the west it adjoins Texas and Oklahoma. The land is a mixture of Mississippi lowlands, rolling prairie, forests, and mountains. It was first visited by the Spaniards, then explored and settled by the French. As part of the Louisiana Purchase, it was sold to the United States in 1803. The Boston Mountains, part of the Ozarks, lie in northern Arkansas, while the Ouachitas, containing Hot Springs National Park, spread across the west of the state. Many vacationers come to bathe in the state's natural spring waters at resorts such as Mammoth Spring and Hot Springs. One of the biggest resort towns, Eureka Springs, is a city cut into the mountainside and has been a resort since 1879. Water temperatures in the springs vary from 95° to 147° F (35° to 63° C). The town has a museum devoted to the temperance (anti-liquor) crusader Carry Nation, famous for smashing up saloons with an ax.

Along with tourism, the state derives much income from its fertile farmland. Food processing is probably the state's most important industry. Before the Civil War, Arkansas was primarily an agricultural state, with many small farms worked by slaves. (During the Civil War Arkansas became a Confederate state.) Today, industry is more important than agriculture. The state is rich in minerals, and is the leading producer of bauxite — used to make aluminum — most of which is mined near the capital, Little Rock, in the center of the state. Oil is mined near El Dorado, and coal and natural gas are produced in the Arkansas valley near Fort Smith. Copper and molybdenum are also mined.

LITTLE ROCK
The skyline of the state's capital and largest city, Little Rock, which lies on the south side of the Arkansas River. The city was home to William E. Woodruff, who founded the *Arkansas Gazette* — the oldest newspaper west of the Mississippi. Important civil rights demonstrations took place here in the 1950s and 1960s.

Pine

Apple blossom

Mockingbird

STATE SYMBOLS

DIAMONDS
Over 60,000 diamonds have been found by visitors to Crater of Diamonds State Park — the only active diamond fields open to the public in the United States. The park lies near Murfreesboro, in the southeast of the state, and the Little Missouri River runs through it.

PETIT JEAN STATE PARK
A spectacular high waterfall dominates the attractive Petit Jean State Park, not far from Little Rock. This river links up with the Arkansas River — itself the longest tributary of the Mississippi–Missouri system. Petit Jean was the nickname of a girl who put on boys' clothing so that she could be with the man she loved in the New World wilderness. The park also has caves and a canyon. The people of Arkansas call their home "the natural state," and the land lives up to its reputation for outdoor enthusiasts. The rivers and streams provide excellent canoeing and white-water rafting, as well as fishing.

ARKANSAS

Capital
Little Rock
Area
53,187 sq. mi
(137,754 sq. km)
Population
2,350,725 (1990)
Largest cities
Little Rock (175,795),
Fort Smith (72,798),
North Little Rock
(61,741)
Statehood
June 15, 1836
Rank: 25th
Principal rivers
Arkansas, Mississippi
Highest point
Magazine Mountain,
2,753 feet (840 m)
Motto
Regnat Populus
(The People Rule)
Song
"Arkansas"

DOUGLAS MACARTHUR

The famous World War II and Korean War general, Douglas MacArthur was born in Little Rock in 1880. In MacArthur Park is the former army arsenal building where he was born. MacArthur organized the defense of the Philippines against the Japanese early in World War II. When he was forced to withdraw his troops, he made a famous promise to the Filipinos: "I shall return." This he did in 1944 as Allied commander in the Southwest Pacific. He liberated the Philippines and supervised the occupation of Japan.

RICE FIELDS

Arkansas is the leading producer of rice in the United States. Many rice fields can be found to the east of Little Rock, around Stuttgart. Wild geese and ducks migrating along the Mississippi River stop at the rice fields to rest. Because there are more of these fields than are now needed for rice, some are put to other uses. A few are flooded to form experimental fish farms. Visitors can see the fish farms and also learn about the farming history of the state at the Stuttgart Agricultural Museum. After rice, the most valuable crop is soybeans. Corn is also grown in most of the state, while in the western highlands farmers grow hay, oats, wheat, and fruit. There are also many dairy farms.

FARMLAND

This is typical farmland in Arkansas, near Fort Smith, close to the state's western border with Oklahoma. Fort Smith itself is a famous historic site, established in 1817 to protect early settlers and covered wagon trains against Native American tribes. In this region crops are grown for about 180 days, but farther south, the growing season lasts for about 240 days a year. Fort Smith lies close to the Arkansas River, which cuts the state almost diagonally in half.

LIZARDS

Reptiles, such as the Eastern fence lizard shown here, thrive in the warm Arkansas wilderness. Lizards are cold-blooded animals, which means they must spend most of the day absorbing warmth from the sun. Arkansas' wooded hills abound with wildlife. Besides lizards, there are many kinds of snake; game birds such as pheasants, quails, and wild turkeys; and mammals such as foxes, deer, and bobcats.

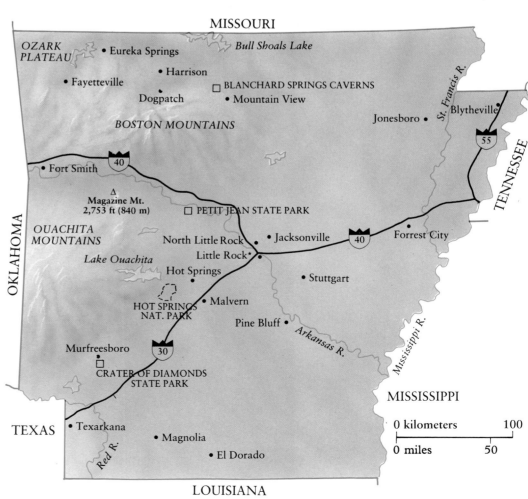

MISSOURI

OZARK PLATEAU
• Eureka Springs
Bull Shoals Lake
• Harrison
• Fayetteville
☐ BLANCHARD SPRINGS CAVERNS
Dogpatch
• Mountain View
Jonesboro •
St. Francis R.
• Blytheville
BOSTON MOUNTAINS
55

• Fort Smith
40

Δ Magazine Mt.
2,753 ft (840 m)
☐ PETIT JEAN STATE PARK

OUACHITA MOUNTAINS
North Little Rock
• Jacksonville
40
• Forrest City
Little Rock *
Lake Ouachita
Hot Springs
• Stuttgart
HOT SPRINGS NAT. PARK
• Malvern
Pine Bluff •
Arkansas R.
Mississippi R.

Murfreesboro
30
☐ CRATER OF DIAMONDS STATE PARK

MISSISSIPPI

0 kilometers   100
0 miles   50

TEXAS
• Texarkana
• Magnolia
• El Dorado
Red R.

OKLAHOMA

TENNESSEE

LOUISIANA

CALIFORNIA

California valley quail

California is the third-largest state. Only Alaska and Texas are larger. It is located on the Pacific coast, and stretches 780 miles (1,260 km) from the Oregon border in the north, to the Mexican border in the south. It has the highest population of any state. Its popular name, the "Golden State," refers to the discovery of gold there in 1848. Today the term could be taken to mean the land of "golden opportunity," for its sunny climate, amazing natural beauty, strong economy, and relaxed lifestyle continue to lure Americans and immigrants alike. Los Angeles is the largest city and the second-largest in the nation. It includes the famous district of Hollywood — the center of the movie world. It is also the city of smog — produced by carbon dioxide emissions from some 8 million automobiles plying along the 10-lane freeways of the Greater Los Angeles area. To the north lies San Francisco. The city has a famous cable car system originally introduced to relieve horses of the difficult job of dragging streetcars up the city's steep hills. Inland from San Francisco lies the Central Valley, with the San Joaquin River providing a source for well-irrigated citrus fruit groves and farms that produce over 200 other agricultural products. California is also a state of natural wonders. At Yosemite National Park you can see the country's highest waterfall, Yosemite Falls, which drops 2,425 feet (740m) in three cascades. Several parks preserve giant redwood trees, many over 300 feet (90m) tall, and some over 3,000 years old. At Inyo National Forest, the bristlecone pines are believed to be 4,600 years old, which makes them the oldest living things on earth. In Death Valley, a barren desert, lies the lowest point in North America at 282 feet (86 m) below sea level.

STATE SYMBOLS

Golden poppy

California redwood

CALIFORNIA

Capital
Sacramento
Area
158, 706 sq. mi
(411,049 sq. km)
Population
29,760,021 (1990)
Largest cities
Los Angeles (3,485,398),
San Diego (1,110,549),
San José (782,248),
San Francisco (723,959)
Statehood
September 9, 1850
Rank: 31st
Principal rivers
Sacramento,
Colorado
Highest point
Mt. Whitney
14,494 ft (4,418 m)
Motto
Eureka (I Have
Found It)
Song
"I Love You, California"

SHROUDED IN CLOUD
The Golden Gate Bridge spans the entrance to San Francisco Bay. It was completed in 1932 and, at 4,200 feet (1,280m), is the second-longest suspension bridge in the country. It is often hidden by morning and evening fog rolling in over the hills.

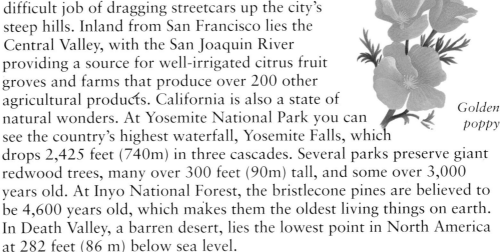

JOHN STEINBECK
Nobel Prize-winning novelist John Steinbeck was born in Salinas. Many of his books, including *The Grapes of Wrath* (1940), are realistic and sympathetic portrayals of poor migrant farm workers in the region. Today, a museum at Salinas houses Steinbeck's manuscripts and photographs, as well as signed editions of his book.

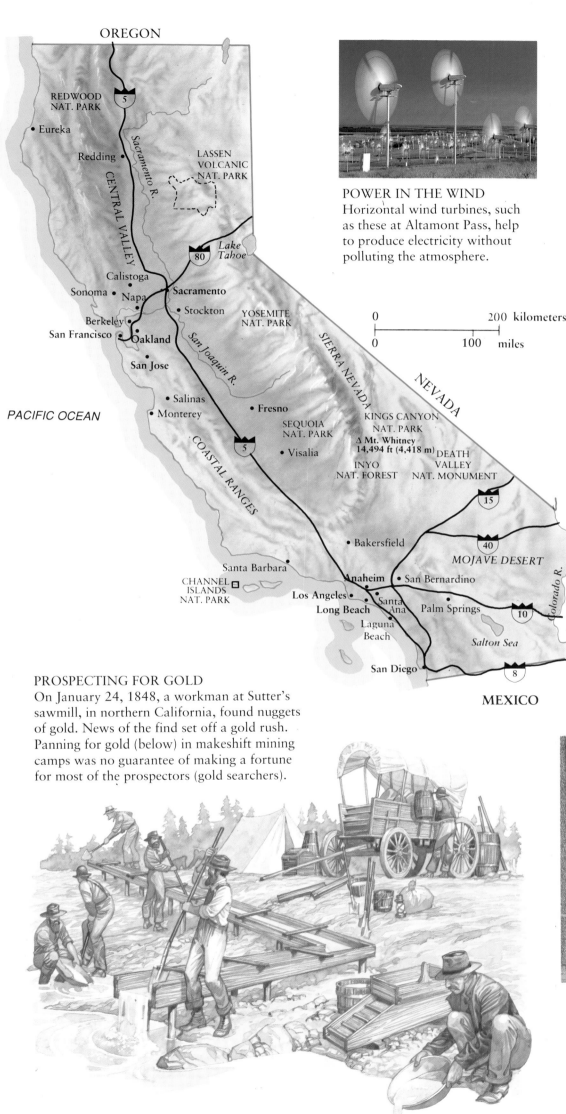

OREGON

REDWOOD
NAT. PARK

• Eureka

Redding •

Sacramento R.

CENTRAL VALLEY

LASSEN
VOLCANIC
NAT. PARK

Lake
Tahoe

80

Calistoga •
Sonoma • Napa •
Berkeley •
San Francisco •
Oakland

Sacramento •
• Stockton

YOSEMITE
NAT. PARK

San Jose

San Joaquin R.

SIERRA NEVADA

NEVADA

5

• Salinas
• Monterey

• Fresno

SEQUOIA
NAT. PARK

KINGS CANYON
NAT. PARK
Δ Mt. Whitney
14,494 ft (4,418 m)

PACIFIC OCEAN

COASTAL RANGES

• Visalia

INYO
NAT. FOREST

DEATH
VALLEY
NAT. MONUMENT

15

• Bakersfield

MOJAVE DESERT

40

Santa Barbara •

CHANNEL
ISLANDS
NAT. PARK

Anaheim •

• San Bernardino

Los Angeles •
Long Beach •

Santa
Ana

• Palm Springs

Colorado R.

ARIZONA

Laguna
Beach

Salton Sea

10

San Diego •

8

MEXICO

0 _____ 200 kilometers
0 _____ 100 miles

POWER IN THE WIND
Horizontal wind turbines, such
as these at Altamont Pass, help
to produce electricity without
polluting the atmosphere.

WEST COAST WINES
The vineyards inland from San Francisco in
the Napa and Sonoma valleys produce most
of the nation's wine. Large vineyards, such as
the Mediterranean-style Sterling Vineyard
(below) at Calistoga, are open for public
tours. There are over 200 wineries in the
region, and the grape harvest takes place
from September into October. Early Spanish
mission padres were the first wine growers.

PROSPECTING FOR GOLD
On January 24, 1848, a workman at Sutter's
sawmill, in northern California, found nuggets
of gold. News of the find set off a gold rush.
Panning for gold (below) in makeshift mining
camps was no guarantee of making a fortune
for most of the prospectors (gold searchers).

LIVING ON THE FAULT LINE
The San Andreas fault (where huge plates of rock
deep in the earth's crust meet) runs 270 miles
(435 km) through west-central California. When
the plates move, they cause earthquakes. Despite
having buildings strengthened against earthquakes,
San Francisco suffered earthquake damage in 1989.

29

COLORADO

There is a certain neatness about Colorado. It became a state in 1876 — 100 years after the signing of the Declaration of Independence — so it is called "the Centennial (100th year) State." It looks like a perfect rectangle on the map, being 387 miles (623 km) long from east to west, and 276 miles (444 km) long from north to south.

Colorado is one of the Rocky Mountain states. More than half of the state is rugged and mountainous, with over 1,000 peaks above 10,000 feet (3,000 m) high. Eastern Colorado is flatter and marks the western edge of the Great Plains. Most of Colorado's population live here, particularly in and around Denver, the capital of the state and also the largest city of the Great Plains. But even Denver lies a mile (1.6 km) above sea level, and the state has the highest elevation in the nation.

The major river in the western United States, the Colorado, has its source in the state, as does the Rio Grande. Towering mountains, mighty rivers, and sprawling plains make Colorado one of the most dramatically beautiful states. Tourism is a major industry, with skiers coming to Vail and Aspen in winter. Another source of income is Colorado's varied mineral wealth — gold, silver, copper, zinc, manganese, molybdenum, coal, lead, and uranium.

Eastern Colorado formed part of the Louisiana Purchase in 1803. Much of the rest of the state comes from territory that was handed over by Mexico after the Mexican War, in 1848.

ANCIENT CLIFF PALACE
Set in the recessed rock, these cliff dwellings were built centuries ago by Native Americans who farmed the local region. This ancient cliff-dwelling civilization flourished from about 500 B.C. to A.D. 1300. These cliff palaces are preserved in the Mesa Verde National Park.

Lark bunting

STATE SYMBOLS

Blue spruce

Rocky Mountain columbine

THE AGRICULTURAL STATE
About half of Colorado is grazing land, and cattle and sheep ranching are primary industries. Cattle raising is the largest source of farm income, and there is much dairy farming. In this picture cattle and sheep graze beneath the snow-covered peaks of the Rocky Mountains. Corn, wheat, hay, and sugar beets are the main crops grown in the state.

COLORADO BEETLE
Colorado beetles, or potato bugs as they are also called, do terrible damage to potato crops. In their natural Rocky Mountain home, they live on a wild plant of the potato family. When early settlers planted potatoes in Colorado, the beetles took to the new crop with relish.

COLORADO	
Capital	
Denver	
Area	
104,091 sq. mi (269,596 sq. km)	
Population	
3,294,394 (1990)	
Largest cities	
Denver (467,610), Colorado Springs (281,140)	
Statehood	
August 1, 1876 Rank: 38th	
Principal rivers	
Colorado, Rio Grande	
Highest point	
Mt. Elbert, 14,433 feet (4,399 m)	
Motto	
Nil Sine Numine (Nothing without Providence)	
Song	
"Where the Columbines Grow"	

MAROON BELL MOUNTAINS
Blue spruce and delicate blue columbines, the state tree and flower, grow in abundance in this area of the Rocky Mountains toward the center of Colorado. Nearby is one of the world's most famous ski resorts, Aspen. Aspen also has a well-known environmental center. Rocky Mountain National Park, in northern Colorado, has more than 100 peaks over 10,000 feet (3,000 m) high.

DENVER SKYLINE
Colorado's capital, Denver, is exactly 5,280 feet (1,600 m) above sea level, so it is known as the Mile-High City. It is the industrial, commercial, and transportation center of the Rocky Mountain region, and its size and importance are reflected by its modern skyscrapers. Denver is also the home of the U.S. Mint, where millions of coins are produced, or minted, each year. There are only two other federal mints in the country.

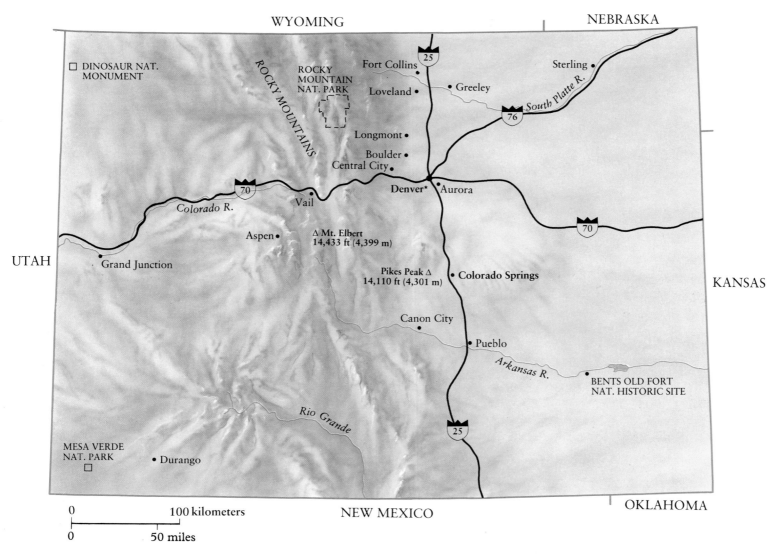

WYOMING

NEBRASKA

□ DINOSAUR NAT. MONUMENT

ROCKY MOUNTAINS

ROCKY MOUNTAIN NAT. PARK

Fort Collins

25

Sterling

Loveland •

• Greeley

South Platte R.

76

Longmont •

Boulder •

Central City •

Denver*

Aurora

70

Vail •

Colorado R.

Aspen •

Δ Mt. Elbert
14,433 ft (4,399 m)

70

UTAH

• Grand Junction

Pikes Peak Δ
14,110 ft (4,301 m)

• Colorado Springs

KANSAS

Canon City •

• Pueblo

Arkansas R.

BENTS OLD FORT
NAT. HISTORIC SITE

Rio Grande

MESA VERDE
NAT. PARK
□

• Durango

25

0   100 kilometers

0   50 miles

NEW MEXICO

OKLAHOMA

CONNECTICUT

Located on the northeastern seaboard, with 250 miles (403 km) of Atlantic coastline, Connecticut is the southernmost of the New England states. It is also the third-smallest in size, and stretches only 95 miles (153 km) from east to west, and 60 miles (97 km) north to south. Two areas of mainly wooded hilly country border a central river valley region. It is a historic state, and its state nickname, the "Constitution State," refers to its system of government, based on what is believed to be the first written constitution in America, dating from the 17th century. Connecticut also has the country's oldest continuously published newspaper, *The Hartford Courant*, the country's first public school, and the first warship, the *Oliver Cromwell*. In 1707 the nation's first copper mine was opened at East Granby. It was later converted by the British into a prison to house enemies of colonial rule.

Connecticut was originally the home of the Pequot tribe of Native Americans. They were defeated by British settlers from Massachusetts in 1637, and the area was one of the first in the United States to be settled by Europeans. The state played an important part in the American Revolution and in the drawing up of the U.S. Constitution. Delegates proposed the Connecticut Compromise, by which all states would have equal representation in the Senate, but representation would be based on population in the House of Representatives — a basis for government which survives today.

STATE CAPITOL
Connecticut's elegant, gold-domed capitol building in Hartford was built in 1879. It contains mementos of the Revolutionary War, and is the meeting place of the state legislature. Across the street, in the State Library building, is housed the table upon which President Abraham Lincoln signed the Emancipation Proclamation, which freed the slaves of the Confederate states.

STATE SYMBOLS

White oak

American robin

Mountain laurel

THE AGE OF SAIL
The reconstructed early 19th-century whaling seaport of Mystic lies on the Mystic River, by Long Island Sound. Connecticut's long shoreline once made it the leading whaling state, as well as supporting a thriving oyster- and lobster-fishing industry. In the 1800s, New England's whaling fleets set sail from ports such as Mystic. Restored sea captains' houses, taverns, shops, and galleries with seafaring treasures line the harbor front, and there are old steamboats and whaling ships to explore — one of which hunted whales for 80 years.

CLASSIC REVOLVER
The famous Colt revolvers which "won the West" were invented and manufactured in Hartford. There are many early rifles and revolvers on view in the city's museums. It was the gun manufacturer Samuel Colt who pioneered the use of interchangeable parts that made mass-production of guns possible.

CONNECTICUT

Capital
Hartford
Area
5,018 sq.mi (12,997sq.km)
Population
3,287,116 (1990)
Largest cities
Bridgeport (141,686),
Hartford (139,739)
Statehood
January 9, 1788
Rank: 5th
Principal rivers
Connecticut, Housatonic
Highest point
Mt.Frissell, 2,380 ft (726m)
Motto
Qui Transtulit Sustinet
(He Who Transplanted
Still Sustains)
Song
"Yankee Doodle"

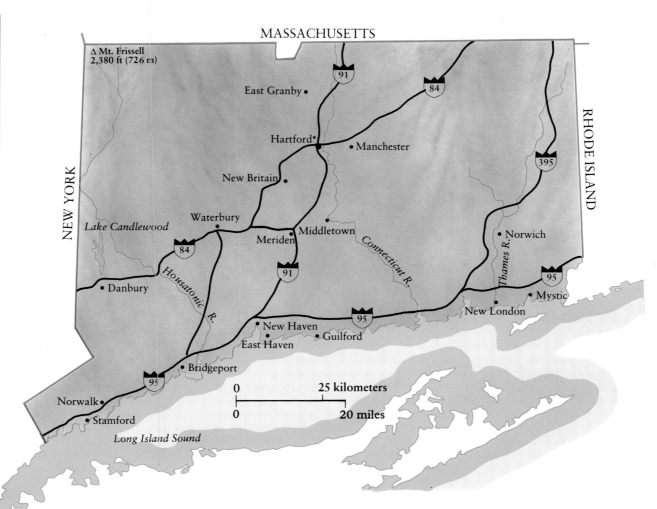

CORN FARM
Although very industrialized, Connecticut is known for its rolling countryside dotted with small farms, such as this one with its field of corn. Sweet corn is the chief vegetable grown in the state. Most of Connecticut's income, however, comes from industry and commerce.

HARRIET BEECHER STOWE
This Connecticut-born author wrote one of the most famous anti-slavery novels, *Uncle Tom's Cabin*. When President Abraham Lincoln met Harriet Beecher Stowe during the Civil War, he said, "So you're the little lady who wrote the book that caused this great war."

YALE UNIVERSITY
One of the nation's great seats of learning, Yale University, is situated in New Haven, Connecticut, near Long Island Sound. It was founded in 1701 and is the third-oldest college in the United States. Until 1969 it was a male-only college. It was named after a wealthy English merchant, Elihu Yale, who made his money from trade in the East Indies. He contributed rare books, and goods from the East Indies, which were sold to raise the money for building the new college. Its library holds six million books and is one of the largest in the country. The university also has an art gallery and a museum of natural history.

DELAWARE

Delaware is nicknamed the "First State" because it was the first to approve the new U.S. Constitution on December 7, 1787. Apart from being the oldest state of the Union, it is also the second-smallest, after Rhode Island. It measures only 96 miles (155 km) from north to south, and 35 miles (56 km) from east to west. Delaware lies on the Atlantic coast between Maryland, Pennsylvania, and New Jersey. The historic Mason-Dixon Line, which fixed the boundary between Maryland and Pennsylvania, also marks Delaware's north-south border with Maryland. Englishman Samuel Argall, of the Virginia colony, sailed up the present Delaware Bay, and named it after Thomas De La Warr, governor of Virginia. In 1638 the New Sweden Company sent out an expedition headed by Peter Minuit to settle the area as New Sweden. Minuit founded Fort Christina, near the present city of Wilmington, the largest in the state. Wilmington still has close ties with Sweden. In 1655 the Dutch conquered New Sweden, but in 1664 the English captured it from the Dutch, renaming it New York. Delaware was formed from part of this colony. The capital, Dover, was founded in 1717. It is one of the oldest and smallest state capitals.

Delaware's industry and economy are closely tied to one family — the Du Ponts.

DELAWARE

Capital
Dover
Area
2,045 sq. mi
(5,297 sq.km)
Population
666,168 (1990)
Largest cities
Wilmington (71,529),
Dover (27,630)
Statehood
December 7, 1787
Rank: 1st
Principal rivers
Delaware, Mispillion,
Nanticoke
Highest point
Centerville,
442 feet (135 m)
Motto
Liberty and
Independence
Song
"Our Delaware"

FISHING FOR A LIVING
Commercial fishing brings in over $4 million a year for Delaware's economy. Menhaden is the chief catch. A type of herring, it provides oil, fish meal, and fertilizers. Freshwater fishing is a popular pastime. Fishermen find bass, carp, catfish, eels, pike, trout, and white perch in Delaware's lakes, ponds, and streams.

American eel

Éleuthère Irénée Du Pont started a firm to make gunpowder in 1802. The Du Pont company no longer makes gunpowder, but it is a world-leading manufacturer of chemicals (Wilmington has been called the chemical capital of the world), plastics, synthetic fibers, dyes, and paints. Delaware is an important business center, with favorable company laws which have attracted hundreds of thousands of U.S. companies to set up corporations in the state — even though they may conduct most of their business elsewhere. Fishing and tourism also aid the state's economy.

Delaware has several wildlife reserves, including the Bombay Hook Wildlife Refuge, a haven for water birds, and the Great Cypress Swamp, the northernmost natural stand of cypress trees in the country.

Pike

Largemouth bass

FARMLAND
Delaware has good soil for farming. In the north of the state are most of the dairy farms and grain farms, such as this one, pictured in winter. Poultry, fruit, and vegetable farming are concentrated in the central and southern areas. The main crops are soybeans, corn, potatoes, and mushrooms. Vegetable and fruit crops include beans, squash, spinach, tomatoes, pumpkins, and melons.

STATE SYMBOLS

American holly

Peach blossom

Blue hen chicken

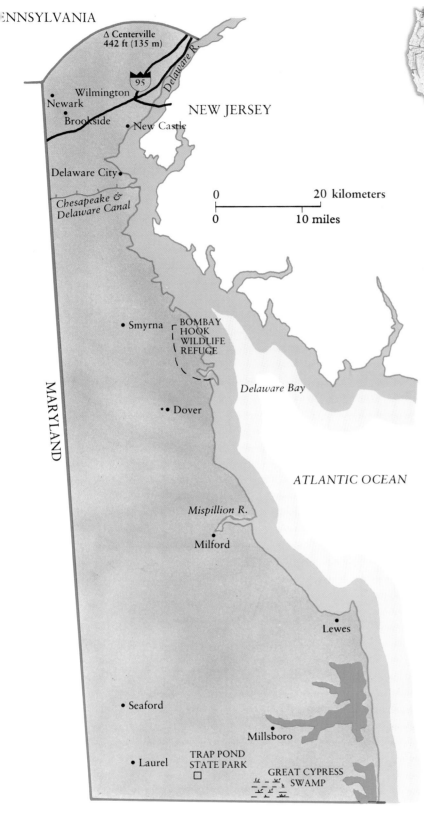

SNAPPING TURTLES
A snapping turtle is well named because it can snap off a person's finger with its powerful jaws should a hand stray too close to it. Snapping turtles and a number of other North American turtles live in fresh water, and are found in Delaware's swamps.

CHICKEN FARMING
Broiler chickens are a major Delaware farm product. Broilers are young chickens, usually 2½ pounds (1 kg) in weight. The chicks pictured here are only two days old. Most poultry farms are in the center and southern parts of the state; they produce more than 225 million broilers a year.

"THE DU PONT STATE"
The Hagley Museum is located on the original site of the Du Pont gunpowder works in Wilmington. The museum complex features restored mills, a water wheel with water turbine, and other machines of the early-1800s. The colonial-style house seen here was built by E. I. Du Pont in 1803. He started the family business that is now the single major corporation in the state. The museum houses antiques from five generations of the family. There are other Du Pont family mansions in Delaware, with beautiful gardens and lavish antiques.

MEMORIAL BRIDGE
A twin road bridge that spans the Delaware River, the Delaware Memorial Bridge joins Delaware to New Jersey south of Wilmington. It is the largest twin-span suspension bridge in the world. Over 60,000 vehicles cross the bridge each day. The Delaware River flows from New York State south through New Jersey and Pennsylvania and then to Delaware. It is 280 miles (450 km) long.

FLORIDA

Florida is the southernmost state on the U.S. mainland and is aptly named the "Sunshine State" — it rarely freezes as far south as Miami. The state's ideal warm climate has made it one of the most popular retirement and vacation spots for people from other states, and from overseas. Three out of four residents originally come from outside the state, an influx which has led to rapid urbanization. Florida has more senior citizens than any other state.

Florida's sunshine has made it the number one orange- and grapefruit-growing state. It is also the leading honey producer, and exports avocados, pomegranates, mangoes, and other exotic fruits. Orange farming began with Spanish settlers in 1536 around St. Augustine — the first permanent European settlement in North America. St. Augustine has a layout that is typical of a 16th-century Spanish city. The center of the state, around Orlando, is now the main area for cultivation. This is also the site for the state's major beef and dairy cattle industry. Orlando is home to the famous Walt Disney World, including the Epcot Center.

Florida has no mountains or high hills. Its low-lying terrain, combined with high humidity and heavy bursts of rainfall, has created many swamps and lakes. The biggest lake is Lake Okeechobee, in the southeast, which covers about 700 square miles (1,800 sq. km). It is the largest lake in the southern United States. Jacksonville, in the northeast corner, is the state's largest city, and the largest in land area in the contiguous United States. The St. Johns River, which runs through the city, is one of the few rivers in the United States that flows from south to north. South of Miami lies the Everglades, which is the largest subtropical wilderness in the mainland United States. It contains the only U.S. mangrove swamps.

SPACE SHUTTLE
Visitors to the John F. Kennedy Space Center, Cape Canaveral, may be lucky enough to witness the launch of a space shuttle. It was from here that the first U.S. manned flight left in 1961, as did the lunar-landing flight on July 16, 1969 carrying Neil Armstrong, the first man on the Moon.

SEA SIRENS
Manatees are mammals, so they must come to the surface to breathe. There are about 1,000 manatees, or seacows, surviving in Florida's waters, where they are a protected species. They can live for up to 50 years.

ISLAND CHAIN
Off the tip of Florida are the Florida Keys. These are a chain of islands and reefs, linked by a central causeway, which form an arc into the Gulf of Mexico. Key West, the southernmost island, provided a working place for American writers Tennessee Williams, John Dos Passos, and Ernest Hemingway. The islands and keys lie only just over 90 miles (140 km) from Cuba.

STATE SYMBOLS

Palmetto palm

Orange blossom

Mockingbird

FLORIDA	
Capital	
Tallahassee	
Area	
58,664 sq.mi	
(151,940 sq. km)	
Population	
12,937,926 (1990)	
Largest cities	
Jacksonville (635,230),	
Miami (358,548),	
Tampa (280,015)	
Statehood	
March 3, 1845	
Rank: 27th	
Principal rivers	
St. Johns, St. Marys,	
Suwannee, Apalachicola	
Highest point	
A hilltop in Walton	
County,	
345 feet (105 m)	
Motto	
In God We Trust	
Song	
"Swanee River"	

HOTEL CHAIN
Some 5 million tourists come annually to the slim barrier island of Miami Beach to visit its hundreds of hotels and one long beach — seen here separated from mainland Miami by Biscayne Bay. Once almost completley eroded, a 10-mile (16-km) stretch of the oceanside beach has been restored with breakwaters and reefs.

GATORS GALORE!
Alligators thrive in the wild subtropical swamplands of Florida. They can grow up to 19 feet (5.8 m) long. They eat fish, frogs, snakes, and even small deer. There are many alligator farms and zoos in the state, and alligators are a protected species.

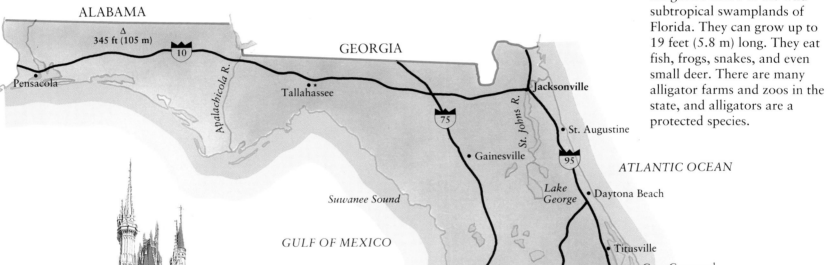

MAGICAL KINGDOM
Walt Disney World includes two vast parks: the Magic Kingdom and the Epcot Center, making up some 360 acres (145 hectares) of activities and entertainment. Both are situated at Orlando in central Florida. The most famous symbol of Walt Disney World is probably Cinderella's Castle (above).

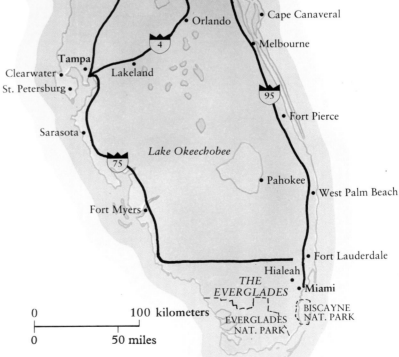

GEORGIA

Located in the southeast corner of the country, to the north of Florida, Georgia is the largest state east of the Mississippi River — almost the same size as the New England states combined. This is one reason for its nickname, "Empire State of the South" — the other being its prosperity. Atlanta, the capital, is the commercial and financial hub of the Southeast.

Georgia's wealth derives chiefly from farming — especially soybeans, peanuts, tobacco, corn, and wheat. Even today many Georgians live on farms and around small towns. Rural Georgia still resembles the old pre-Civil War South, with its economy based on staple crops, though cotton is no longer the major crop. The peaches for which Georgia is famous are still grown, but mainly along its Atlantic coast.

The Blue Ridge Mountains rise in northeastern Georgia, a region of dense pine forests. Besides providing valuable timber, this region attracts hunters, fishermen, and tourists. West of these mountains lies the fertile Appalachian Valley, and to the south is the Piedmont, a plateau where Atlanta is situated, together with many large farms. The plateau drops to the coastal plain — the largest part of the state, and which includes Okefenokee Swamp. The swamp is now a wildlife refuge.

Georgia was founded in 1733 by James Oglethorpe, who named the colony in honor of King George II of England. Before his arrival, Creek and Cherokee Indians lived in the area, and Spanish and French explorers had arrived in the 1500s. The state has seen both Revolutionary War and Civil War battles, and was badly damaged during the Civil War. In the 1960s Georgia was greatly involved in the civil rights movement, led by Martin Luther King, Jr.

Live oak

Cherokee rose

Brown thrasher

STATE SYMBOLS

SOLDIERS SET IN STONE
Confederate war heroes Jefferson Davis, Robert E. Lee, and Stonewall Jackson are carved into the light-gray granite of Stone Mountain, near Atlanta. They stand some 90 feet (27 m) high, by 190 feet (58 m) wide. Stone Mountain itself is the largest smooth-sided rock dome in North America, and measures 2 miles (3.2 km) long by 1 mile (1.6 km) wide.

ATLANTA
Once called Terminus, because it stood at the southern end, or terminus, of a major rail network, Atlanta remains the transportation center of the state. Its airport is the third-busiest in the nation. It is also the state capital, largest city, and center of Georgia's thriving textile industry. The skyscrapers signal that this is a modern, industrial city, yet it has not forgotten its Southern heritage.

A TREE-LINED STATE
The Blue Ridge Mountains in northeast Georgia are covered with pine trees. Forests once extended over the whole state, and even today 70 percent, or 103,596 square miles (268,314 sq. km) of Georgia is covered with trees. The state ranks first in the growth of timber. Pine trees yield pulpwood, which is used to produce paper.

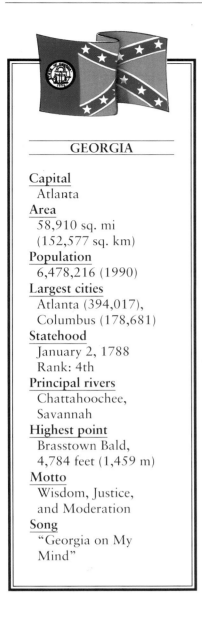

GEORGIA

Capital
Atlanta

Area
58,910 sq. mi
(152,577 sq. km)

Population
6,478,216 (1990)

Largest cities
Atlanta (394,017),
Columbus (178,681)

Statehood
January 2, 1788
Rank: 4th

Principal rivers
Chattahoochee,
Savannah

Highest point
Brasstown Bald,
4,784 feet (1,459 m)

Motto
Wisdom, Justice,
and Moderation

Song
"Georgia on My
Mind"

VAST SWAMP
Spanish moss hangs from the semi-submerged
trees in Okefenokee Swamp, at the southern end
of Georgia. The swamp is the largest freshwater
swamp in the United States, and contains the
Okefenokee National Wildlife Refuge. Alligators,
bears, raccoons, and many birds are among the
animals protected there. The swamp was once part
of the Atlantic Ocean, but is now around 100 feet
(30 m) above sea level.

NOT A NUT, BUT A PEA
Georgia is the largest peanut-growing state, and
the United States is one of the world's leading
producers of this vegetable. Peanuts are eaten not
only as a snack, but also in foods such as peanut
butter and peanut brittle. Peanuts can be crushed
for oil as well as for use in many products
including shampoo and even paint. They are also
used to feed livestock.

MARTIN LUTHER KING
The Reverend Martin Luther King,
Jr., born in Atlanta in 1929, was
the nation's most famous black
civil rights activist. He aimed to
promote political, social,
educational, and economic rights
for black people through non-
violent demonstrations. Martin
Luther King was assassinated in
1968, four years after receiving the
Nobel Prize for Peace.

HAWAII

The youngest and most tropical state of the United States, Hawaii is the only one that does not lie on the North American mainland. It is a chain of 132 volcanic islands in the Pacific Ocean — the only state to be made up entirely of islands — lying about 2,400 miles (3,900 km) southwest of San Francisco. This also makes it the most southerly state, and Hilo, on the island of Hawaii, is the southernmost city in the United States.

The islands are the peaks of huge underwater volcanoes. After Hawaii, the largest island, the other major islands in order of size are Maui, Oahu, Kauai, Molokai, Lanai, Niihau, and Kahoolawe. Almost 80 percent of the people live on Oahu, many of them in and around Honolulu, the state's capital.

Tourism is the main source of prosperity, and millions of Americans flock to Hawaii to enjoy the warm climate, the coral reefs, sandy beaches, surfing waves, lush, tropical mountain scenery, and relaxed, friendly lifestyle. The word *Aloha*, from which the state gets its nickname, means "love" in the Hawaiian language (whose alphabet has only 12 letters). The weather is not always sunny; in fact Mt. Waialeale, on Kauai, has the highest annual rainfall in the United States. Such a wet environment is ideal for the cultivation of subtropical crops such as sugar cane and pineapples. The original Hawaiians were Polynesians, who sailed to the islands over 2,000 years ago in great canoes. Today they make up only one percent of the population. Many residents have come from Japan, the Philippines, China, and other parts of of Asia. Captain James Cook was probably the first European to reach Hawaii in 1778. In the 1820s many missionaries from the United States began to settle there. Hawaii became a U.S. territory in 1900.

Nene (Hawaiian goose)

Hibiscus

STATE SYMBOLS

Kukui (Candlenut)

BEACH OF DREAMS
Waikiki Beach, near Honolulu on Oahu, is one of the most popular tourist attractions in the United States. It has become somewhat spoiled by its own popularity, with over-development of hotels and crowded beaches. With the hottest and coolest days of the year differing in temperature by as little as 10°F (5°C), the beaches of Hawaii provide recreation all year round. The famous Diamond Head promontory, in the background, is an extinct volcanic crater. Near the beach are the yacht harbor and Kapiolani Park.

DECEMBER 7, 1941
"A date which will live in infamy," said President Franklin D. Roosevelt, referring to the Japanese aerial attack on Pearl Harbor, which caused heavy losses and crippled the U.S. fleet during World War II. However, many damaged warships were salvaged, and the base was quickly repaired to become the headquarters of the U.S. war in the Pacific. A memorial, built over the partly-submerged battleship *Arizona*, which sank with more than 1,000 sailors, honors the dead. Pearl Harbor was an important base in both the Korean and Vietnam wars.

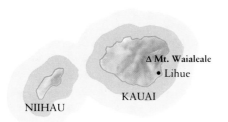

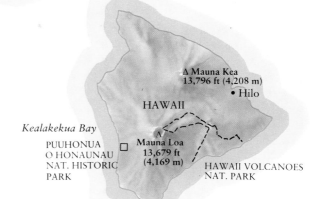

- Mt. Waialeale
- Lihue

NIIHAU KAUAI

OAHU
- Haleiwa
Wahiawa - Kaneohe
Pearl City - Kailua
- Honolulu
Pearl Harbor

PACIFIC OCEAN

MOLOKAI

MAUI
Wailuku -
Lahaina - Kahului

0   50 kilometers
0   50 miles

LANAI

HALEAKALA NAT. PARK

KAHOOLAWE

Mauna Kea
13,796 ft (4,208 m)
- Hilo

HAWAII

Kealakekua Bay

PUUHONUA
O HONAUNAU
NAT. HISTORIC
PARK

Mauna Loa
13,679 ft
(4,169 m)

HAWAII VOLCANOES
NAT. PARK

HAWAII

Capital
Honolulu

Area
6,471 sq. mi
(16,760 sq. km)

Population
1,108,229 (1990)

Largest cities
Honolulu (365,272),
Hilo (37,808)

Statehood
August 21, 1959. Rank: 50th

Principal river
Wailuku (Hawaii)

Highest point
Mauna Kea,
13,796 ft (4,208 m)

Motto
Ua Mau Ke Ea O Ka Aina I Ka Pono
(The Life of the Land is Perpetuated in Righteousness)

Song
"Hawaii Ponoi"

THE FIRST HAWAIIANS
Polynesian children pose for the camera. They are direct descendants of the first settlers, who sailed to Hawaii from islands in the western Pacific between A.D. 300 and 750. The first schools were founded by missionaries in the 1840s.

LAVA FLOW
The Hawaiian Islands were formed by volcanoes over millions of years. They rise up from the Pacific Ocean floor, as deep as 18,000 feet (5,500 m). Hawaii has the largest active and inactive volcanoes in the world. Haleakala, on Maui, is the largest inactive volcano — its crater measures 33 square miles (85 sq. km). It rises just over 10,000 feet (3,000 m) and the crater's interior is home to the rare silversword plant. Massive Mauna Loa, on Hawaii, is one of the most active volcanoes, and threatens nearby human settlements.

PRICKLY FRUIT
Pineapples are an important crop in Hawaii. Although not native to the islands, they thrive there, and the state is the world's biggest exporter of the fruit. Pineapple plantations were started in the 1800s, and by the end of the century were making their owners wealthy. High yields are maintained by the use of irrigation and machinery for both planting and harvesting. Most canned pineapple used in the United States comes from Hawaii. Sugar cane, however, is the main export.

41

IDAHO

Nicknamed the "Gem of the Mountains" to describe its stunning scenic beauty, as well as its natural wealth in gemstones and precious metals, Idaho is a large northwestern state. When it was made a territory in 1863, it was even larger than Texas, but Montana and Wyoming were later taken away from the territory, leaving the state of Idaho with its current rank as the 13th-largest state in the Union.

Much of Idaho is mountainous: the Bitterroot Range includes the Salmon River Mountains, which rise up in the central part of the state, and the Clearwater Mountains, which extend north to Canada. This latter range forms part of the Rocky Mountains. Idaho has a curious, somewhat house-like shape, with a "chimney" abutting the Canadian border. Its low population, about one million, gives it a density of only 12 people to every square mile. Over 70 percent of the people live within 30 miles (50 km) of the Snake River, in the south of the state. This is also where Idaho's farmlands are located, and the irrigated fields of volcanic soil along the river are the planting grounds not only for the famous Idaho potatoes, but also for wheat, sugar beets, and barley. Idaho raises more potatoes — and more commercial trout — than any other state. Most crops are transported through the capital and largest city, Boise, which lies on a branch of the Snake River. Sheep and cattle raising are also important in this area. Tourism, skiing, and other outdoor activities, such as hunting and trekking, provide a growing income.

The first white settlers in what were Nez Percé and Shoshone Indian lands were fur traders and Jesuit missionaries, who arrived in the 1830s. In the 1860s Mormons set up Idaho's first permanent settlement. A gold rush occurred at the same time, and more settlers arrived, forcing the Indians to give up their land.

Mountain bluebird

STATE SYMBOLS

Syringa

Western white pine

BOOM AND BUST
Silver City Ghost Town is a relic of Idaho's mining boom from the 1860s. Although it also had a gold rush, Idaho became the leading silver producer in the United States, until the falling price of silver forced many mines to close. There are many old gold- and silver-mining ghost towns, such as Centerville, Placeville, and Pioneerville.

IDAHO
Capital
Boise
Area
83,564 sq. mi
(216,430 sq. km)
Population
1,006,749 (1990)
Largest cities
Boise (125,738),
Pocatello (46,080)
Statehood
July 3, 1890
Rank: 43rd
Principal rivers
Snake, Salmon,
Clearwater
Highest point
Borah Peak,
12,662 ft (3,859 m)
Motto
Esto perpetua
(It is Forever)
Song
"Here We Have
Idaho"

LEWIS AND CLARK EXPEDITION
The famous American explorers Meriwether Lewis and William Clark were the first whites known to pass through this region, en route from St. Louis, Missouri, to the Pacific Ocean in 1805. They traveled via the Bitterroot Range, through a pass in what is now Montana. The two men were greatly helped by local Indians, particularly the Nez Percé and the Shoshone. A Shoshone woman, Sacagawea, gave messages of peace to the Indian tribes Lewis and Clark met. They also exchanged gifts as a gesture of goodwill. The explorers collected plant and mineral specimens on their 4,000-mile (6,400-km) journey.

MOOSE
The largest member of the deer family, the moose lives in northern woodlands near water. With its long legs it can wade through swamps or pick its way through snowy forests. Once moose lived throughout the northern United States, but nearly all the moose in the east were killed by hunters. Moose are now protected by law.

WHITE-WATER RAFTING
A kayak on the Salmon River, which twists and cuts its way through the Salmon River Mountains on its way west to the Snake River. The Salmon is the longest river within any state. River rafters shoot the rapids of this "river of no return" — so called because there is no turning back in the swift current. Such outdoor adventure sports attract thousands of visitors to Idaho's unspoiled acres.

A STATE OF MANY FALLS
Rivers, particularly the Snake River, are a prominent feature of Idaho's landscape. The Snake River rushes westward, its journey punctuated by cascades, such as this spectacular one at Shoshone Falls. Many of the state's names feature the word "falls", such as Idaho Falls, Twin Falls, and American Falls. The Snake River runs through Hell's Canyon, the deepest gorge in North America, and far deeper than the Grand Canyon.

IDAHO POTATO
No other state compares with Idaho in potato production. The lava-rich soils that drain southward from the Snake River provide fertile growing ground for this important food of the western world. The potato originated in South America and was introduced to North America in the 1600s.

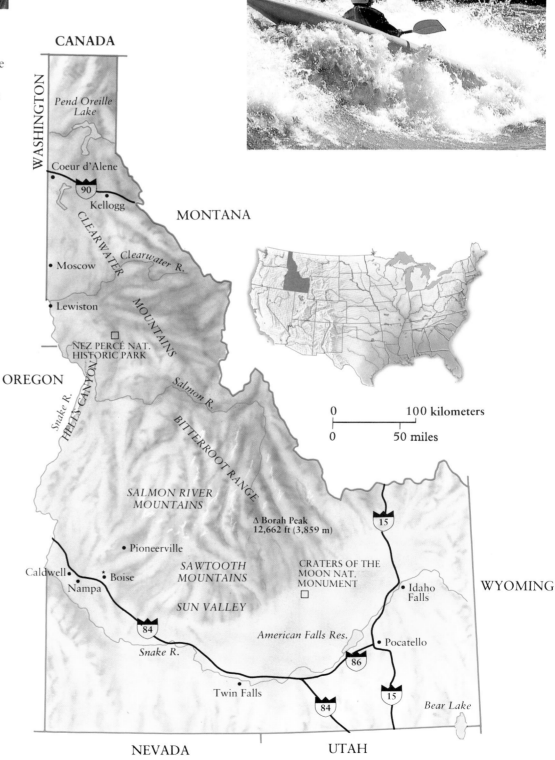

CANADA

WASHINGTON

Pend Oreille Lake

Coeur d'Alene

90

Kellogg

MONTANA

CLEARWATER MOUNTAINS

Clearwater R.

Moscow

Lewiston

NEZ PERCÉ NAT. HISTORIC PARK

OREGON

Snake R.

HELLS CANYON

Salmon R.

BITTERROOT RANGE

SALMON RIVER MOUNTAINS

△ Borah Peak 12,662 ft (3,859 m)

Pioneerville

Caldwell

Boise

Nampa

SAWTOOTH MOUNTAINS

SUN VALLEY

CRATERS OF THE MOON NAT. MONUMENT

15

Idaho Falls

WYOMING

84

American Falls Res.

86

Pocatello

Snake R.

Twin Falls

84

15

Bear Lake

NEVADA

UTAH

0   100 kilometers
0   50 miles

ILLINOIS

Located in the heart of the Midwest, Illinois typifies that region's broad, level landscape — hence its popular name, the "Prairie State." The fertile soil and long growing season make it an important agricultural state. It is among the leading producers of soybeans and corn. Wheat, oats, barley, rye, and sorghum are also grown in large quantities. Hogs, pigs, and cattle are important to the state's economy. Illinois is also a major industrial state; in fact, manufacturing is much more vital to Illinois than farming, and products include electronic equipment and chemicals. Chicago, the largest city in Illinois and home of O'Hare Airport, is a major center for rail and truck transportation, as well as for the Great Lakes shipping traffic. There is mining in the southern part of the state. During the 1800s and early 1900s, Illinois' factories and stockyards were the workplaces where many of America's labor unions first formed.

White oak

The Mississippi forms the western border of the state from Galena — home of General Ulysses S. Grant and endowed with many restored Victorian buildings — to Cairo in the south. Evidence of Illinois' prehistoric inhabitants is plentiful. There have been dwellers on the plains since 4000 B.C., and a period of burial mound building began after about 1000 B.C. Monk's Mound, one of the Cahokia Mounds, in the southwest of the state near East St. Louis, is the largest Indian mound in the country. The name "Illinois" comes from the tribes that once lived in the area. They called themselves Illinewek, or "superior men." French fur traders were the first European settlers in the early 1600s.

Cardinal

STATE SYMBOLS

Illinois native violet

HOME OF LINCOLN
Springfield, near the center of the state, was home to the young lawyer, congressman, and finally president, Abraham Lincoln. The town cemetery holds his tomb. At the village of New Salem there is a state park which honors his time there as a store-tender, law student, and surveyor.

CHICAGO SKYLINE
Chicago is the third–largest city in the United States and the birthplace of the skyscraper. The John Hancock Center in the middle of the picture is one of the city's tallest buildings. The Sears Tower (not shown) is the world's tallest building at 1,454 feet (443 m).

ILLINOIS

Capital
Springfield
Area
56,345 sq. mi
(145,933 sq. km)
Population
11,430,602 (1990)
Largest cities
Chicago (2,783,726),
Rockford (139,426)
Statehood
December 3, 1818
Rank: 21st
Principal rivers
Mississippi, Ohio,
Illinois, Wabash
Highest point
Charles Mound,
1,235 ft (376 m)
Motto
State Sovereignty —
National Union
Song
"Illinois"

FOOD OF THE FUTURE
A typical farm with its crop of soybeans (foreground) and corn. More soybeans are grown in Illinois than in any other state. The town of Decatur has the label "soybean capital of the world." The soybean is also the second most important crop — after corn — for the whole of the United States. Corn accounts for some 58 percent of total crop produce, while soya makes up nearly 15 percent.

MISSISSIPPI BARGES
Barges with up to 50 containers travel slowly along the Mississippi River, the "Father of Waters," near Cairo, in the south of the state. Thus, Chicago serves as a shipping crossroads between the Great Lakes and the Gulf Coast. The Mississippi runs along Illinois' western border. The Illinois River links it to Lake Michigan via the Illinois Waterway.

WHITE-TAILED DEER
The white-tailed deer is the most common deer in North America. The open country of the Illinois plains suits its habits, and it can run at 40 miles per hour (64 km/h) to avoid predators. As with all deer, it is the male that has the antlers. The deer eats leaves, fruit, and grass, as well as the bark of trees.

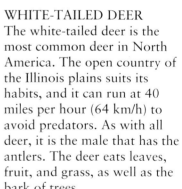

CARL SANDBURG
The poet, historian, and folklorist Carl Sandburg was born in Galesburg in 1878. He became famous for his poetic descriptions of gritty American life. Sandburg was a popular folk singer and made a collection of songs, *The American Songbag*, in 1927. He wrote a famous six-volume biography of Abraham Lincoln and also wrote children's books.

INDIANA

Rich in farmlands, Indiana ranks among the top-ten agricultural states of the Union. It is also an important industrial state. Its motto as "Crossroads of America" is well earned — it is a major Midwest road, rail, river, lake, and canal transportation center. In the northwest it borders Lake Michigan, and this lakefront area has much industry. Shipping carries goods from the lake, via the St. Lawrence Seaway, to other U.S. and overseas markets. The Ohio River forms the state's southern border and flows into the Mississippi, allowing the state's produce to be carried on to New Orleans. Farmland makes up 80 percent of the state, and almost 95 percent of Indiana's produce is sent to other parts of the country. Corn is the chief crop, but soybeans and wheat are also grown. Hogs and pigs, cattle, and chickens are raised. There are also valuable tracts of forest.

Industry began in the 1800s with coal mines and quarries, followed by oil refineries, steel mills, and factories, which are concentrated around Gary, Fort Wayne, and South Bend in the north. Indiana's industrialization has caused pollution problems over the years, but laws now attempt to control the damage and safeguard wild areas on Lake Michigan's shoreline. For example, visitors can explore the windswept dunes and forests of the Indiana Dunes National Lakeshore, at the crescent of Lake Michigan. Indiana got its name from the many Indian tribes that once lived there. In the early 1800s these tribes fought a number of fierce battles with the U.S. Army. At Tippecanoe in 1811, General William Henry Harrison defeated the Miami Indians and cleared the way for a permanent European settlement. The nickname "Hoosier" state is harder to attribute. The most likely explanation relates to Samuel Hoosier, who was working on the Ohio Falls Canal at Louisville, Kentucky, in 1826. He preferred to hire men from across the river in Indiana, and "Hoosier's men" came to mean reliable workers, from whom the state may have taken its nickname.

STATE SYMBOLS

Tulip tree

Cardinal

Peony

CITY OF WHEELS
At the dead center of the state, Indianapolis is both the state's capital and its largest city. Major highways emerge from the city like spokes from a wheel, and Indianapolis has more major highway connections than any other city in the United States. At the center of the city stands the tall Soldiers and Sailors Monument in World War Memorial Plaza. Nearby is the state capitol building (below).

SMELL BARRIER
Widespread over North America, skunks dwell in dens and burrows over much of Indiana's prairie land. The skunk has two white stripes down its black, furry body, and a thin white line on its face. Its distinctive appearance should warn off most attackers; but should they provoke it they will be overpowered by the fluid it sprays from its tail-end glands. Only owls are serious predators, because they can swoop on skunks before the release of the fluid, which can be sprayed to over 6 feet (2 m). Skunks come out chiefly at night to forage.

INDIANA
Capital
Indianapolis
Area
36,185 sq. mi
(93,719 sq. km)
Population
5,544,159 (1990)
Largest cities
Indianapolis (731,327),
Fort Wayne (173,072)
Statehood
December 11, 1816
Rank: 19th
Principal rivers
Ohio, Wabash,
White
Highest Point
Wayne County,
Franklin Township,
1,257 feet (383m)
Motto
Crossroads of America
Song
"On the Banks of the
Wabash, Far Away"

RACE OF CHAMPIONS

"Gentlemen, start your engines" heralds the start of the annual Indianapolis 500 auto race, held some 5 miles (8 km) west of the downtown area. The Motor Speedway track is 2½ miles (4 km) in circumference. The race is held over the Memorial Day weekend and hundreds of thousands of visitors swell the city for the event. Indianapolis also holds a traditional Memorial Day parade. Visitors to the city can take a special bus ride around the world-famous track and then go on to visit displays of antique racing cars.

WOODCHUCK

The woodchuck is a member of the squirrel family, and is found in wooded areas, including the forests of southern Indiana. It is about 25 inches (65 cm) long, with a bushy tail and sharp-clawed feet, which help it to dig its underground burrows: hence its other name of groundhog. It feeds on grass, leaves, shoots, seeds, and fruit.

MILES OF CORN

Indiana's number-one crop is corn, and this contributes to the state's standing as a top-ten farming producer. There are over 85,000 farms, which are highly mechanized. Those farms which belong to the Amish and Mennonite sects, devout Christians who settled in Indiana in the 1800s, preserve older traditions of farming. Their farms are located in the north of the state, around Berne and Goshen. Other crops include sorghum, oats, rye, and hay. Tomatoes, spearmint and peppermint are all important crops.

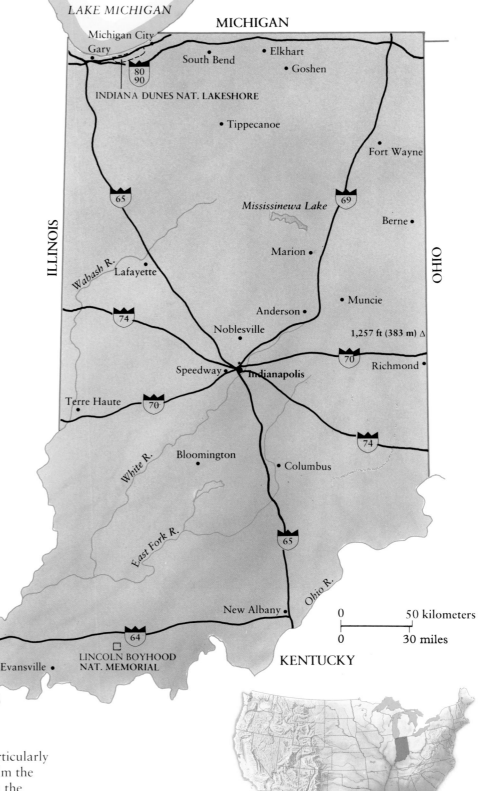

BRIEF OFFICE

William Henry Harrison was the ninth president, but his term of office lasted barely one month in 1841. While delivering his Inaugural Address, he caught a cold, which later turned into pneumonia. His success against the Indians, particularly at the battle of Tippecanoe, won him the election. He was the president with the shortest term, and the first to die in office.

IOWA

A rich farming state of the Midwest, Iowa competes with Illinois for first place in growing corn, and raises more pigs and hogs than any other state. It ranks third in cattle production. Around 90 percent of the state is farmland. One reason for Iowa's high output of agricultural crops is its gently rolling land: its soil, mostly black loam and rocks, is fertile — deposited by melting glaciers at the end of the last Ice Age. Once the crops and livestock leave the farms they contribute to Iowa's considerable industrial output as factories turn them into meat, cereals, animal feeds, and other processed food products. Farm machinery is another key industry. The eastern border of Iowa is the Mississippi River, while its western border is formed by the Big Sioux and Missouri rivers. The Mississippi and Missouri, which eventually converge just north of St. Louis, Missouri, are important to Iowa as a key agricultural state. These rivers provide irrigation water in case of drought, as well as serving as waterways for shipping bulk goods, such as grain, to other parts of the country.

The first Europeans to see Iowa were probably French explorers and fur trappers. Iowa was part of the land included in the Louisiana Purchase of 1803. In 1832 an uprising of Sauk (or Sac) and Fox tribes, led by Black Hawk, attempted to oust the Europeans but was defeated, and more settlers filled the region. It became a U.S. territory in 1838. Iowa's nickname, "Hawkeye," probably honors Black Hawk.

At Iowa City there is the University of Iowa and the original state capitol, dating from the time when the state was admitted to the Union. Iowa is also home to seven villages called the Amana Colonies, founded in the 1850s. This German religious sect sought religious freedom, and their descendants continue a tradition of making woolens, furniture, wine, and baked goods.

GILDED DOMES
Iowa's Capitol Building in Des Moines has gold-leafed domes that dominate the surrounding area. The building took 15 years to complete (in 1886). Nearly 30 types of marble went into its ornate construction. Inside the building are murals and mosaics. The annual State Fair is held in Des Moines in August.

Oak

STATE
SYMBOLS

Eastern goldfinch   *Wild rose*

ALFALFA AND CORN FIELDS
A farm in Iowa with corn and alfalfa crops growing side by side. The state's leading position in farming, both nationally and internationally, is based on the feeding (as well as selling) of livestock. Corn and alfalfa provide important food for cattle. Alfalfa is a plant of the pea family which originated in the Middle East. Today the Midwest states, particularly Iowa, produce the most alfalfa in the world.

DEPRESSION PRESIDENT
Herbert Clark Hoover was born in West Branch, Iowa, where his birthplace has been restored as a historic site. During his term of office, from 1929 to 1933, the United States experienced the worst economic depression in its history. Hoover was blamed for not doing enough to help the poor and jobless. He died in 1964.

SOYA

Originally from China and Japan, the soybean was introduced to the United States at the start of the 1800s, and established its place in the Midwest. The soya plant is upright and leafy, growing up to 6 feet (2 m) high, and lives for only one year. It produces a number of pods, which contain one to four seeds, or beans.

THE MIGHTY MISSISSIPPI

The Mississippi River runs its powerful course at Guttenberg, on the eastern border of Iowa. Much of the state is rolling — rather than flat — countryside. There are also many bluffs along the river banks of both the Mississippi and Missouri rivers. Bluffs are high, steep banks or cliffs. The Mississippi River irrigates the fertile farms along its banks and provides barge and other boat transportation for the state's farm produce.

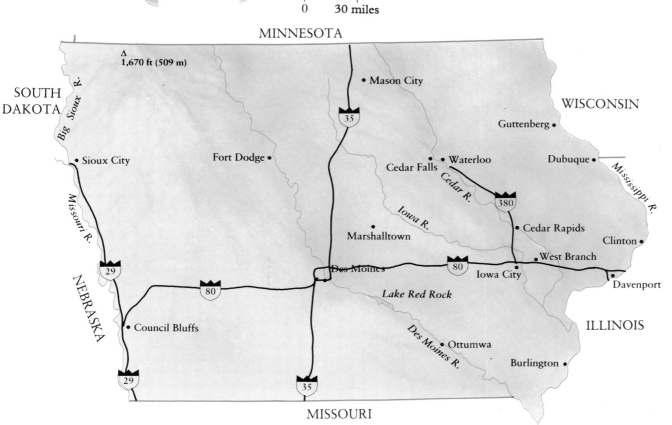

0   50 kilometers

0   30 miles

IOWA

Capital
Des Moines
Area
56,275 sq.mi
(145,472 sq.km)
Population
2,776,755 (1990)
Largest cities
Des Moines (193,187),
Cedar Rapids (108,751)
Statehood
December 28, 1846
Rank: 29th
Principal rivers
Missouri, Mississippi
Highest point
Osceola County,
1,670 feet (509 m)
Motto
Our Liberties We Prize
and Our Rights We
Shall Maintain
Song
"The Song of Iowa"

HOG FARMING

Iowa has often ranked second in terms of overall value of its livestock, and the state produces about 25 percent of the nation's pigs with 13.5 million hogs and nearly 30 million pigs. Hogs are pigs that weigh over 120 pounds (50kg). Corn is the pigs' main food and Iowa produces that, too, in abundance. More than two-thirds of the nation's pigs are raised in the corn belt states of the Midwest. There are about 53 million pigs on U.S. farms, made up of some 20 breeds. Spotted swine, American landrace, and Poland china are among the breeds raised commercially.

KANSAS

The state of Kansas lies at the very center of the continental United States. There is a monument to acknowledge this fact just outside Lebanon, Smith County, in north-central Kansas. A few miles from here the state song, "Home on the Range," was written. As with the other Midwest states, farming plays a major part in the Kansas economy, and large farms dominate the flat central plain. The farming wealth of Kansas comes from its rich soil, made fertile over millions of years as it developed out of an inland sea. Wheat, sorghum, and corn are grown on this flat and fertile land. Meat packing is also important. In the east there are rolling hills, and in the west the state steepens slowly to become part of the Great Plains which rise toward the Rocky Mountains. Kansas is the number one wheat growing state. It is also the leading sorghum producer, and the state's grains, along with grains from other states, are stored in huge grain silos. There are 200 million bushels of grain held in the storage silos of Wichita and Topeka. Both these cities are also heavily industrialized.

The Spanish explorer Francisco Vásquez de Coronado was the first European to see Kansas, while searching unsuccessfully for gold in 1541. There were also many Native American tribes in the region, including Wichita, Pawnee, Osage, and Kansa — from which the state gets its name. Kansas formed part of the Louisiana Purchase of 1803, when Napoleon sold his North American territories to President Thomas Jefferson. In 1825 a treaty was made to allow safe passage across Osage Indian land for pioneers taking their wagons on the Santa Fe Trail. Two years later the first army post west of the Mississippi, at Fort Leavenworth, was opened to protect both settlers and pioneers from Indian attacks. Before the Civil War, the state became the scene of such violence between pro- and anti-slavery groups that it was called "Bleeding Kansas." Kansas developed quickly after the Civil War, especially as the railroad came to Wichita, Abilene, and Dodge City — centers of the "Wild West." Soon cowboys were driving cattle up from Texas to catch these railheads. Kansas has been a leading state in developing women's political rights. Susanna Salter became the country's first woman mayor in 1987.

Western meadowlark

Cottonwood

STATE SYMBOLS

Sunflower

KANSAS

Capital
Topeka
Area
82,277 sq. mi
(213,097 sq. km)
Population
2,477,574 (1990)
Largest cities
Wichita (304,011),
Kansas City (149,767)
Statehood
January 29, 1861
Rank: 34th
Principal rivers
Kansas, Republican,
Smoky Hill, Arkansas
Highest point
Mt. Sunflower
4,039 feet (1,232 m)
Motto
Ad Astra per Aspera
(To the Stars through
Difficulties)
Song
"Home on the Range"

WHERE THE BUFFALO ROAM
Millions of American bison — usually called buffalo, although they are not true buffaloes — once roamed the Midwest plains and prairies. They were hunted by Native Americans. Later, white hunters using rifles slaughtered some 50 million bison. Today they are protected in National Parks.

AIR CAPITAL
Kansas is a leading state in the manufacture of aircraft. Wichita owes much of its past growth to its aircraft industry. Commercial, private, and military planes have been made here — among them such well-known names as Boeing, Lear, and Cessna. The picture shows Lear jets in production. There is also a major air force base at Wichita.

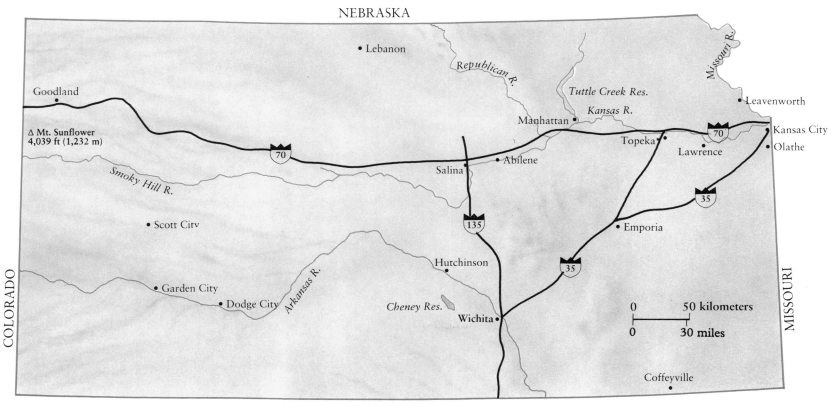

NEBRASKA

Lebanon

Republican R.

Missouri R.

Goodland

Tuttle Creek Res.

Kansas R.

Leavenworth

△ Mt. Sunflower
4,039 ft (1,232 m)

Manhattan

Topeka

70

Kansas City

70

Lawrence

Olathe

Smoky Hill R.

Salina

Abilene

35

COLORADO

Scott City

135

Emporia

MISSOURI

Arkansas R.

Hutchinson

35

Garden City

Dodge City

Cheney Res.

0   50 kilometers

0   30 miles

Wichita

Coffeyville

OKLAHOMA

MONUMENT ROCKS
Modern reminders of the Ice Age glaciers that once swept over the plains and covered most of Kansas, these oddly-shaped formations are called Monument Rocks. They are situated near Scott City and are over 10,000 years old.

GRAIN HARVEST
Kansas ranks first among the states in wheat production. Its soil is among the most fertile in the world, and tall grain elevators and combine harvesters are common sights on the flat, rural landscape. Wheat farming on a large scale really took off in the 1880s, after the ranching cattle boom died down.

PILOT AND PIONEER
The famous American aviator Amelia Earhart was born in Kansas in 1897. She became the first woman to fly alone across the Atlantic in 1932. In 1937 she and a navigator attempted to fly around the world, but her plane was lost in the Pacific Ocean, with less than one-third of her journey to finish.

COWBOY COUNTRY
Dodge City, in the southwest of the state, has many restored store fronts, saloons, wagons, and stagecoaches from its infamous Wild West frontier days. During the 1870s and 1880s longhorn cattle were driven up from Texas by cowboys to the railroad here. The city also attracted businessmen, cattle rustlers, stagecoach robbers, and saloon belles. Frontiersmen such as Wyatt Earp and Doc Holliday once strolled along the boardwalks of this cowboy capital.

KENTUCKY

Situated between the South and the Midwest, Kentucky is the oldest state west of the Appalachians — a mountain chain that has dominated both the state's geography and its history. Nearly a quarter of the state is part of the Appalachian Plateau — also called the Eastern Coal Field.

The Appalachians formed a barrier to westward expansion for the original 13 Atlantic seaboard colonies. People knew that there was land to the west, but getting past the mountains was the problem. The best-known pioneer was Daniel Boone, who blazed the Wilderness Trail through what is now called the Cumberland Gap in the mountains in 1775. The area is now part of the Cumberland Gap National Historic park (shared with Tennessee and Virginia). With 20,222 acres (8,190 hectares) it is the nation's largest historic park. The gap is a natural break about 800 feet (245 m) below the peaks. Nearby, Pinnacle Overlook has commanding views of the mountains and valleys. The borders of the three states meet at Tri-State Peak. The Daniel Boone National Forest contains the Red River Gorge. After Boone's exploration, many white settlers followed, clearing trees and farming hemp, corn, hogs, rye, and tobacco. Today tobacco, soybeans, wheat, and bluegrass are among the leading crops.

Bluegrass, from which the state gets its nickname, has bluish-green blades and is a food source for livestock, and for the famous horses of Kentucky. The state ranks first in the breeding of thoroughbred horses, and the Kentucky Derby is held each year in Louisville. "Bluegrass" is also a term used to describe the local country music. One product for which the state is famous worldwide is Kentucky bourbon whiskey — a drink that is made from corn. Other manufactured items include trucks and automobiles, food products, and chemicals. Kentucky was the birthplace of the two opposing Civil War presidents — the Union's Abraham Lincoln and the Confederacy's Jefferson Davis.

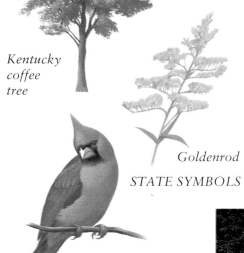

Kentucky coffee tree

Goldenrod

Cardinal

STATE SYMBOLS

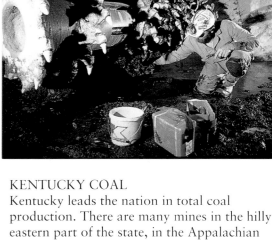

KENTUCKY COAL
Kentucky leads the nation in total coal production. There are many mines in the hilly eastern part of the state, in the Appalachian plateau. The coal mined in this area is a hardened, highly-valued variety called anthracite, which is widely used in industry. Much of the region has suffered from the effects of strip mining and large-scale felling of trees. This is now controlled by law, but much damage remains. Other minerals in the state include petroleum, natural gas, and iron ore.

KENTUCKY		

Capital
Frankfort
Area
40,410 sq mi
(104,662 sq. km)
Population
3,685,296 (1990)
Largest cities
Louisville (269,063),
Lexington-Fayette
(225,366)
Statehood
June 1, 1792
Rank: 15th
Principal rivers
Ohio, Mississippi,
Cumberland, Kentucky
Highest point
Black Mountain,
4,145 feet (1,263 m)
Motto
United We Stand,
Divided We Fall
Song
"My Old Kentucky Home"

CUMBERLAND FALLS
These impressive falls, also known as Great Falls, are part of the Cumberland River, which flows through eastern Kentucky and Tennessee. They drop 68 feet (21 m). The river frequently floods in winter and spring, but is low-level in summer. It flows on to the Ohio River. The Cumberland Gap, Plateau, Falls, and River were all named after the Duke of Cumberland, the son of King George I of England.

THE KENTUCKY DERBY

One of the most famous horse races in the world is the Kentucky Derby. It is held every year on the first Saturday in May at Churchill Downs, Louisville. There are some 300 thoroughbred horse farms in the area around Lexington, which has the excellent blue-green pastures of bluegrass for grazing. These horses, highly prized for their superior quality, are sold all over the United States and around the world.

"THE GREATEST"

Native Kentuckian Muhammad Ali (originally named Cassius Clay) was born in Lexington in 1942. He is the only boxer to win the world heavyweight title three times. He won an Olympic Gold Medal in 1960, and went on to dominate boxing, calling himself "the Greatest."

TRADITIONAL WAYS

The Shakers are a small religious sect who follow a very simple way of life. This is reflected in their traditional farming methods and particularly in their distinctive furniture, which is world famous for its simple, well-made shapes. The Shaker village at Pleasant Hill, established in the 1800s, is near the first permanent English settlement west of the Allegheny Mountains, at Harrodsburg.

OHIO RIVER

To the north of the state, the Ohio River separates Kentucky from Ohio, Indiana, and Illinois. The river is itself a tributary of the Mississippi, and more water flows from it into the Mississippi than from any other tributary.

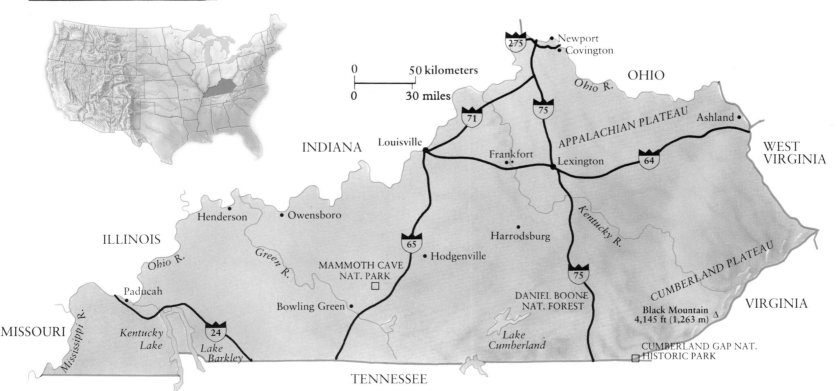

LOUISIANA

Located on the Gulf of Mexico, Louisiana is the lowest-lying state, averaging only 100 feet (30 m) above sea level. Its flatness causes problems along the Gulf coast, which is below sea level and requires dikes, levees, and pumping stations to protect the land from flooding. It is also mainly rural, with large areas of swamps and sluggish marshes called bayous. Many pelicans live in these marshes, and these birds give Louisiana its nickname. The Mississippi River has played an important role in the state's history and economy. Louisiana's three largest cities — New Orleans, Baton Rouge, and Shreveport — are all located on the river. The river also forms part of the state's eastern border with the state of Mississippi, before entering the Mississippi Delta. Louisiana's industry includes petroleum and natural gas, ranking second only to Texas in their production. There are large reserves of both off the coast. It is also the number one salt-producing state. Soybeans, sugarcane, and rice are the leading crops. Louisiana also leads all the other states in its fish industry, which mainly consists of shellfish.

Louisiana's culture is unique, chiefly because of its French origins. Although the Spanish explorer Hernando de Soto sailed there in 1541, the region was claimed for France in 1682 by La Salle. The whole area eventually formed the Louisiana Purchase of 1803. The early French and Spanish settlers were known as Creoles, and their culture is still strong. So too is Cajun cooking, music, and language — the legacy of some 4,000 French people forcibly relocated in the late 1700s by the British from Acadia, their home in Nova Scotia, Canada. The word "Acadian" became shortened to Cajun. In addition, many Africans were brought to Louisiana in the 1700s and 1800s as slaves both from Africa and via the Caribbean.

NEW ORLEANS
This city is unlike any other in the United States. Its ornate wrought-ironwork balconies are an attractive feature on the many buildings from the Spanish and French colonial era. New Orleans is famous for its French Quarter, with restaurants serving spicy Creole cooking and entertainers performing in the streets. Its many cafés offer the traditional half chicory coffee, half hot milk drink.

DIXIELAND JAZZ
The French Quarter of New Orleans is considered the birthplace of jazz — a form of music developed from a mixture of African and Southern influences. Here in the early 1900s, the first jazz marching bands played in the streets at funerals, weddings, and elections. They then moved indoors to clubs, restaurants, and halls, such as Preservation Hall. One of the great jazz trumpeters and singers, Louis Armstrong (third from left in the picture), played with King Oliver's Creole Jazz band in the 1920s in New Orleans.

Brown pelican

STATE SYMBOLS

Bald cypress

FRENCH FOUNDER
French explorer Robert Cavelier Sieur de La Salle, sailed down the Mississippi with a party of French and Native Americans. On April 9, 1682, on reaching the mouth of the river, he claimed all the land in the Mississippi Basin for France. He called the land Louisiana after the French king, Louis XIV. La Salle was the first European to travel the length of the Mississippi River. In 1684, he returned to the Americas to found a colony at the river's mouth, but he was murdered by mutineers before he reached the Mississippi.

Magnolia

LOUISIANA

Capital
Baton Rouge
Area
47,752 sq. mi
(123,678sq. km)
Population
4,219,973 (1990)
Largest cities
New Orleans (496,938),
Baton Rouge (219,531)
Statehood
April 30, 1812
Rank: 18th
Principal rivers
Mississippi, Red,
Sabine
Highest point
Driskill Mountain,
535 feet (163 m)
Motto
Union, Justice, and
Confidence
Song
"Give Me Louisiana"

MARDI GRAS
February (or sometimes March) is the time
for Mardi Gras, which is French for "Fat
Tuesday" and refers to the custom of
using up all the fats in the home before
Lent begins. Its origins lie in the Roman
Catholic tradition of celebrating the day
before Ash Wednesday, the beginning of
Lent. In New Orleans this has become an
extravagant parade of costumed
merrymakers dancing, singing, and
marching through the streets.

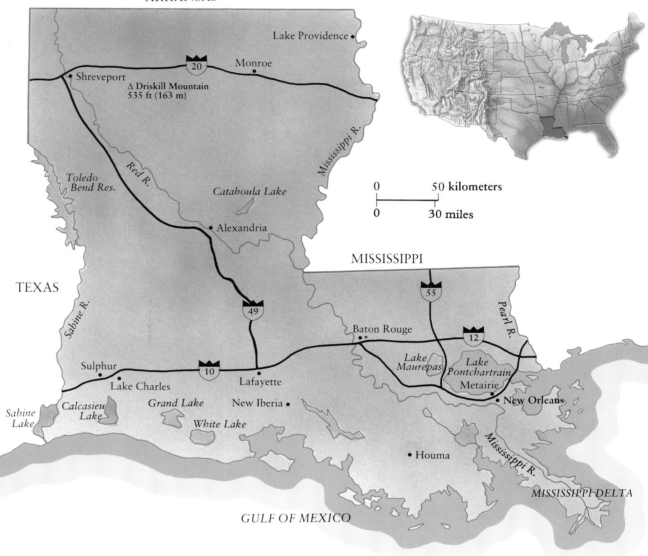

SOURCES OF SULFUR
Hot liquid sulfur spews out of a
pipe from a mine at the aptly
named town of Sulphur. Sulfur,
or sulphur, is found in large
deposits along the coast of the
Gulf of Mexico. It is located in
salt deposits, which are drilled
from special wells. Some sulfur
is extracted from below the
ocean floor. Other sulfur is
recovered from the mining of
natural gas and oil. It is stored
in huge vats. Sulfur is an
industrial mineral that is used
in many compounds.

CRAYFISH COOKING
Louisiana is the leading state in
commercial fishing, particularly of
shellfish. Much of the catch is
exported to other parts of the
United States, but there is also
a strong tradition of local
seafood cooking, particularly
with crayfish. The crayfish is
related to the lobster, and both
are caught near the shore. Many are
caught in freshwater lakes and
swamps by bayou shrimp boats.

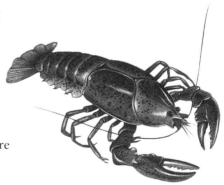

55

MAINE

The most easterly of all the states in the country, Maine is also the largest state in New England. It forms the northeastern corner of the United States, and is bordered by the Canadian provinces of New Brunswick and Quebec, as well as by New Hampshire. The state has a long and rocky coastline on the Atlantic Ocean. Maine is a thinly populated state. It was originally part of Massachusetts but broke away in 1820. The state is naturally divided into two types of landscape — the coastal lowlands and the mountain plateau. The rugged, tree-lined coast has plenty of bays, sandy beaches, and natural harbors, which make it ideal for fishing. Maine seafood, especially lobster, is world famous. Herring and cod are also important catches. Sport fishermen are attracted by sea bass, salmon, and trout. Maine grows enough potatoes to be counted among the top producers in the country of this vegetable. Other crops are corn, hay, blueberries, and apples. Paper production is the leading industry. Footwear, electrical and electronic equipment, machinery, and textiles are other important manufactured goods.

Tourists come to view the rugged and rock-bound coastline, as well as the wildlife in the many national parks, including the Rachel Carson Wildlife Refuge. Carson was a nature writer who warned of environmental dangers. She lived at Kennebunkport, a summer resort which also boasts the summer house of George Bush. It is possible that the Vikings may have reached Maine as far back as A.D. 1000. John Cabot explored the coast for England in 1498 — only six years after Columbus's first voyage to the New World.

STATE SYMBOLS

Chickadee

Eastern white pine

White pine cone & tassel

FARMLAND
Situated in the center of Maine, the forest highlands of Baxter State Park form the backdrop to this rolling farmland and typical New England village, with its single-spired churches. There is no large-scale farming in the state, but potatoes are grown in this region, as are apples, blueberries, and other fruit. Mt. Katahdin, the state's highest peak, is situated in Baxter State Park. The northern end of the Appalachian Trail is also located there, and the area attracts hikers and campers.

AUGUSTA
The state capital, Augusta, is a dynamic city. Here a boat race further enlivens the busy riverfront. The city is the hub of commerce and industry. Plymouth colonists established a fort here in 1628. A later fort, Fort Western (1754) has been restored for visitors.

LIGHTHOUSE
Maine's coastline is dotted with old lighthouses, such as Nubble Lighthouse on Cape Neddick, which were built to warn clippers and whalers away from the perilous rocky shore. It is also along this shoreline that the most easterly point in the United States is located: at West Quoddy Head, a small peninsula near Lubec.

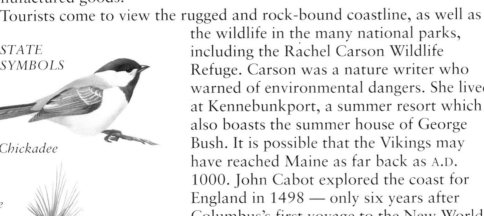

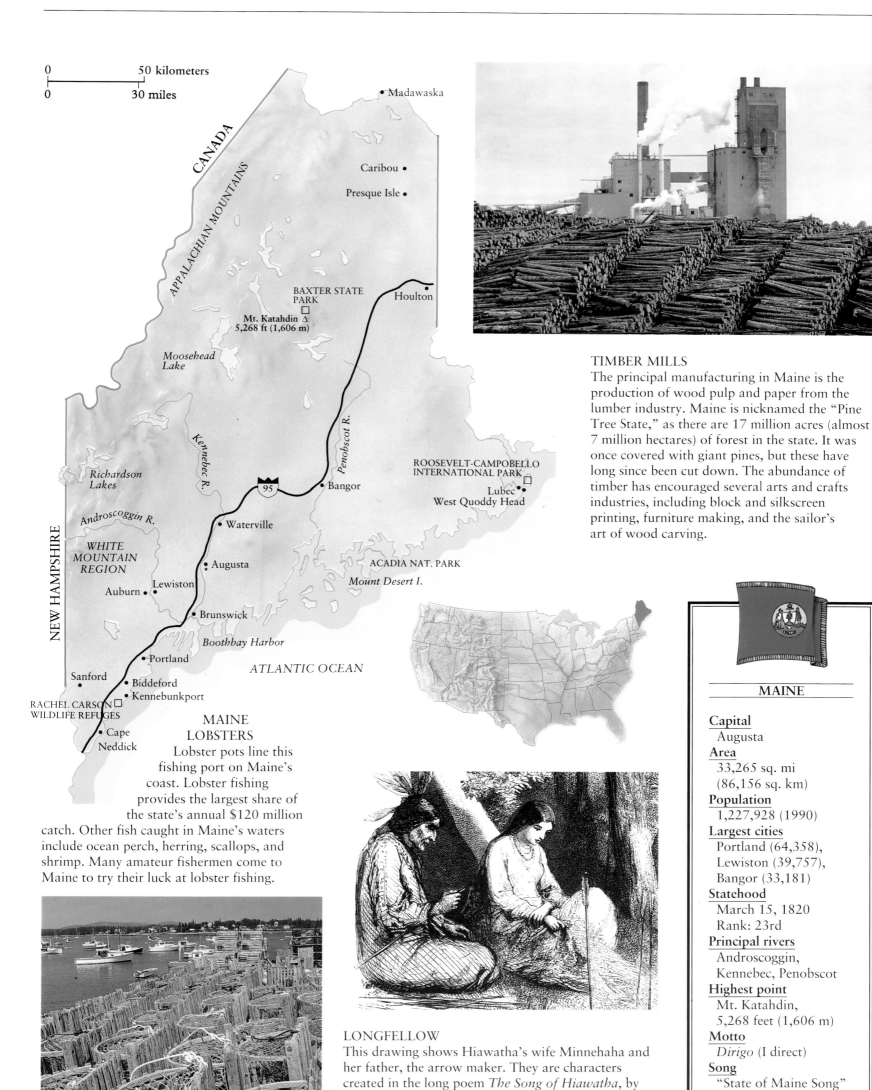

0   50 kilometers

0   30 miles

CANADA

• Madawaska

APPALACHIAN MOUNTAINS

Caribou •

Presque Isle •

BAXTER STATE
PARK

Houlton •

Mt. Katahdin △
5,268 ft (1,606 m)

*Moosehead
Lake*

Kennebec R.

Penobscot R.

95

Bangor •

ROOSEVELT-CAMPOBELLO
INTERNATIONAL PARK

Lubec •
West Quoddy Head

*Richardson
Lakes*

Androscoggin R.

WHITE
MOUNTAIN
REGION

NEW HAMPSHIRE

• Waterville

• Augusta

Auburn •

Lewiston •

ACADIA NAT. PARK
Mount Desert I.

• Brunswick

Boothbay Harbor

ATLANTIC OCEAN

• Portland

Sanford •

Biddeford •
Kennebunkport •

RACHEL CARSON
WILDLIFE REFUGES

• Cape
Neddick

TIMBER MILLS

The principal manufacturing in Maine is the production of wood pulp and paper from the lumber industry. Maine is nicknamed the "Pine Tree State," as there are 17 million acres (almost 7 million hectares) of forest in the state. It was once covered with giant pines, but these have long since been cut down. The abundance of timber has encouraged several arts and crafts industries, including block and silkscreen printing, furniture making, and the sailor's art of wood carving.

MAINE
LOBSTERS

Lobster pots line this fishing port on Maine's coast. Lobster fishing provides the largest share of the state's annual $120 million catch. Other fish caught in Maine's waters include ocean perch, herring, scallops, and shrimp. Many amateur fishermen come to Maine to try their luck at lobster fishing.

LONGFELLOW

This drawing shows Hiawatha's wife Minnehaha and her father, the arrow maker. They are characters created in the long poem *The Song of Hiawatha*, by Henry Wadsworth Longfellow. The poet was born in Maine in 1807, and wrote this epic poem of an Indian brave who becomes the leader of his people.

MAINE

Capital
Augusta

Area
33,265 sq. mi
(86,156 sq. km)

Population
1,227,928 (1990)

Largest cities
Portland (64,358),
Lewiston (39,757),
Bangor (33,181)

Statehood
March 15, 1820
Rank: 23rd

Principal rivers
Androscoggin,
Kennebec, Penobscot

Highest point
Mt. Katahdin,
5,268 feet (1,606 m)

Motto
Dirigo (I direct)

Song
"State of Maine Song"

MARYLAND

A Mid-Atlantic state, Maryland is divided into two parts — the Eastern and Western shores — by Chesapeake Bay. Although it is one of the smallest states, Maryland ranks in the top ten in wealth. Its highly urbanized areas of Baltimore and the suburbs of Washington, D.C., both on the Western Shore, contribute to that prosperity. Most of the state's income comes from manufacturing electric and electronic equipment, chemicals, and food processing. Maryland is also a state of great natural diversity despite its small size. The Chesapeake Bay and Atlantic coastline contrast sharply with the river valleys, mountains, forests, and rolling hills of the interior.

Maryland was first explored by Captain John Smith in 1608. Twenty-four years later, in 1632, King Charles I gave this land to George Calvert, Lord Baltimore, whose son Cecil founded the first settlement, St. Mary's City, in 1634. He named the colony in honor of Queen Henrietta Maria and established it as a place where his fellow Roman Catholics could enjoy freedom of worship. Members of other faiths were also welcomed — their rights guaranteed by an "Act Concerning Religion," passed in 1649, which made Maryland the first colony to officially practice religious toleration.

Although little of the fighting in the Revolutionary War took place in Maryland, its "troops of the line" fought with special valor, earning praise from General Washington and so giving the state its nickname of the "Old Line State." In the War of 1812, the British bombardment of Fort McHenry, in Baltimore Harbor, inspired Francis Scott Key (imprisoned on a British ship) to write the words of "The Star-Spangled Banner."

Although Maryland was a slave state, it was never dominated by large plantations, and it remained in the Union during the Civil War. It also witnessed some of the fiercest fighting of the war. The Battle of Antietam, near Hagerstown, was one of the bloodiest — over 23,000 men were killed.

Annapolis, the capital, has the oldest state capitol (1779) still in use. It is also the site of the United States Naval Academy. President Jimmy Carter was one of its graduates.

MARYLAND	
Capital	Annapolis
Area	10,460 sq. mi (27,091 sq. km)
Population	4,781,468 (1990)
Largest cities	Baltimore (736,014), Rockville (44,835)
Statehood	April 28, 1788 Rank: 7th
Principal rivers	Susquehanna, Potomac
Highest point	Backbone Mountain, 3,360 feet (1,024 m)
Motto	*Fatti Maschii, Parole Femine* (Manly Deeds, Womanly Words)
Song	"Maryland, my Maryland"

BABE RUTH
George Herman "Babe" Ruth was one of baseball's best-loved stars. He was born in 1895 in Baltimore (his birthplace is open to visitors). Babe Ruth began his professional career as a pitcher in 1920, but it was for batting that he was famous. He hit a career total of 714 home runs, unbeaten until 1974.

STATE SYMBOLS

Baltimore oriole

White oak

CHESAPEAKE BAY
An important inlet of the Atlantic Ocean, Chesapeake Bay splits Maryland in two. The bay is 200 miles (320 km) long and is surrounded by Virginia and Maryland. "Chesapeake" is an Algonquian word meaning "country on a big river." The Susquehanna, the Potomac, and several other rivers run into the bay. Baltimore, Maryland, and Norfolk, Virginia, are the two most important ports on the bay. With its many inlets, the bay is a popular vacation spot, offering excellent sailing and fishing. It provides both Maryland and Virginia with an abundance of seafood, especially crabs and oysters.

Black-eyed Susan

BALTIMORE
The most important city of Maryland, Baltimore, is renowned as a seaport and shipbuilding center and industrial base.

MARYLAND CRABS
Crabs form a large part of Maryland's fishing industry. Fishing in the state's tidal waters for crabs and other species is a favorite pastime and requires no license. Maryland restaurants are renowned for their crab dishes.

HARRIET TUBMAN
Born a slave in 1820 in Maryland, Harriet Tubman was called "The Moses of her People" because she helped fellow slaves escape the plantations along the Underground Railroad. This was not a real rail track, but a code name for an escape route. She helped over 300 escape.

TOBACCO HARVEST
Tobacco is grown widely in Maryland, mainly in the southern part of the Western Shore. After the tobacco is picked, as shown here, it goes to the loose-leaf tobacco auctions in the state, which are the largest in the world. Other Maryland crops are corn, soybeans, melons, apples, and peaches. About 40 percent of the land is cultivated. The Eastern Shore is known for its poultry, eggs, and market gardening. Another 40 percent of the land is forested, and so timber, too, is also a major industry.

Map labels:
PENNSYLVANIA
Cumberland
Hagerstown
83
ANTIETAM NAT. BATTLEFIELD SITE
Aberdeen
WEST VIRGINIA
Frederick
HARPERS FERRY NAT. HISTORIC PARK
△ Backbone Mt. 3,360 ft (1,024 m)
70
Baltimore
270
95
Patapsco R.
Rockville
95
VIRGINIA
Potomac R.
Annapolis
WASHINGTON D.C.★
Susquehanna R.
DELAWARE
ATLANTIC
OCEAN
Patuxent R.
Cambridge
Salisbury
Lexington Park
Leonardtown
St. Marys City
ASSATEAGUE ISLAND NAT. SEASHORE
Chesapeake Bay
DELMARVA PENINSULA

0 kilometers 50
0 miles 30

MASSACHUSETTS

Located on the northeastern coast of the United States, the New England state of Massachusetts is bordered on the north by Vermont and New Hampshire. It is one of the smallest states, being only 47 miles (76 km) from north to south at its western end, but it has more inhabitants than any other New England state. Most of the people live in the Greater Boston area. The state is steeped in colonial and revolutionary history. The second permanent English settlement (after Jamestown, Virginia) was established there at Plymouth by the Pilgrims in 1620. It was these Pilgrims who started the American celebration of Thanksgiving Day. The Boston Massacre and Boston Tea Party took place there, and the first shots of the Revolutionary War rang out at Lexington and Concord in 1775. Benjamin Franklin, John Adams, and Paul Revere were all born in Massachusetts.

At the center of the state lies rich farmland irrigated by the Connecticut River, which flows north to south. These farms produce cranberries and many vegetables, as well as milk and eggs. West of the river are the beautiful Berkshire Hills which border New York State. Massachusetts is a major industrial state, and witnessed the start of the country's industrial revolution with the establishment of the nation's first textile factory at Waltham in the 1800s. Today, the state's factories produce textiles that are shipped throughout the entire country, as well as electric and electronic equipment, metal products, books, and other printed material. The state also has a large fishing industry with catches of haddock, flounder, cod, and clams. Massachusetts is famous for its educational establishments, including Harvard University and M.I.T. (Massachusetts Institute of Technology). It is also a major tourist attraction for its historic sites and popular coastal resorts.

American elm

STATE SYMBOLS

Chickadee

Mayflower

MAYFLOWER
At Plimoth Plantation, near the site of Plymouth where the Pilgrims landed in 1620, there is a reconstruction of the Pilgrims' village, with "villagers" enacting day-to-day routines, and a replica of the *Mayflower* — the ship that brought them. Visitors can see their living conditions and imagine the hardships of the voyage.

FIRST U.S. COLLEGE
Harvard University, located in Cambridge, Massachusetts, was founded in 1636. It was named after a Puritan minister, John Harvard, who left to the college his books and considerable funds. The library is now the largest of any U.S. university with over 10 million books. Six American presidents educated there include Franklin D. Roosevelt and John F. Kennedy. Other graduates include Ralph Waldo Emerson, T.S.Eliot, and Norman Mailer. Harvard was founded as a liberal arts and theological college, but later widened its scope to include law, medicine, and science.

THE BOSTON MASSACRE
On March 5, 1770, angry colonists gathered outside the Customs House in Boston and protested against the presence of British troops in the city. They taunted the British guards with cries of "lobster-backs" (after the red coat of a soldier on duty) and hurled snowballs. More soldiers arrived with fixed bayonets, and one soldier opened fire. Five colonists were shot. The resulting "massacre" as it came to be called, was a key event in the developments leading to the Revolutionary War.

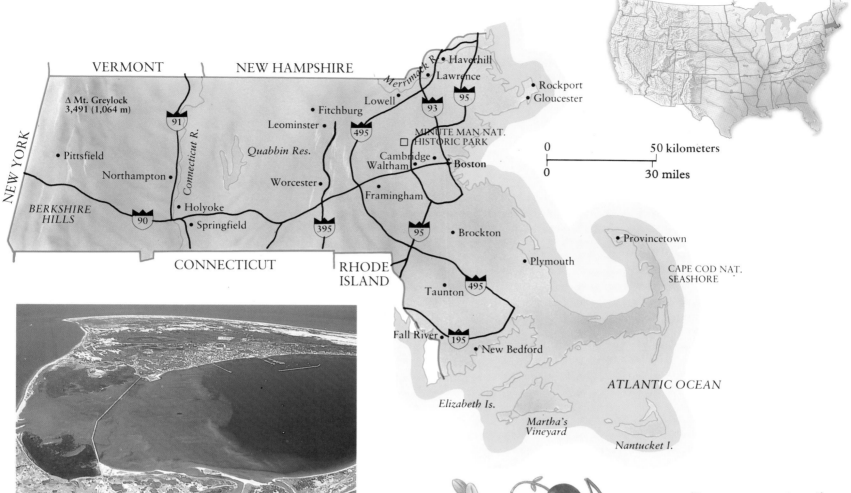

VERMONT NEW HAMPSHIRE

Δ Mt. Greylock
3,491 (1,064 m)

NEW YORK

Pittsfield

Northampton

BERKSHIRE
HILLS

Holyoke

Springfield

Connecticut R.

Leominster

Quabbin Res.

Fitchburg

Lowell

Worcester

Cambridge
Waltham

Framingham

Merrimack R.

Haverhill

Lawrence

93

95

MINUTE MAN NAT.
HISTORIC PARK

Boston

Rockport
Gloucester

Brockton

CONNECTICUT

RHODE
ISLAND

Taunton

Fall River

195

New Bedford

Plymouth

Provincetown

CAPE COD NAT.
SEASHORE

ATLANTIC OCEAN

Elizabeth Is.

*Martha's
Vineyard*

Nantucket I.

0   50 kilometers

0   30 miles

THE LURE OF CAPE COD

Cape Cod is a large peninsula that hooks around like a curled finger for 65 miles (105 km) into the Atlantic Ocean. This aerial view shows Provincetown at the top, with the sandy beach where the Pilgrims first touched land in the foreground. South of it are the Atlantic island resorts of Martha's Vineyard, Nantucket Island, and the Elizabeth Islands. Tourists are a major source of income for the state, and many visitors are drawn there by the beauty of the Cape Cod National Seashore.

CULTURAL CENTER

Boston is only the 20th-largest city in the United States, but many regard it as the first seat of learning, culture, and the arts. Historically it is unrivaled for its preserved colonial attractions. The Freedom Trail, a marked walking tour along the streets takes the visitor past such places as the Boston Massacre site, Benjamin Franklin's birthplace, and Paul Revere's house. In the 1800s Boston became a great port and industrial center. It is home to the world-famous Boston Symphony Orchestra, and the Museum of Fine Arts, with its collection of antiquities and traditional arts.

CRANBERRIES

The cranberry bogs, shallow marshes on Cape Cod, make Massachusetts the leading cranberry producer. Farmers flood the bogs each winter to protect the crops from frost.

MASSACHUSETTS

Capital
Boston

Area
8,284sq.mi (21,455sq.km)

Population
6,016,425 (1990)

Largest cities
Boston (574,283),
Worcester (169,759)

Statehood
February 6, 1788
Rank: 6th

Principal rivers
Connecticut, Charles

Highest point
Mt. Greylock,
3,491 feet (1,064 m)

Motto
Ense Petit Placidam Sub Libertate Quietem (By the Sword We Seek Peace, but Peace Only Under Liberty)

Song
"All Hail to Massachusetts"

MICHIGAN

The state of Michigan is made up of two peninsulas facing each other across the waters of Lake Michigan. The Upper Peninsula and Lower Peninsula, as they are called, do not in fact touch, but are linked by the 5-mile (8-km) long Straits of Mackinac Toll Bridge. The state also borders three other Great Lakes — Superior, Huron, and Erie. The Lower Peninsula, which has been dubbed the "mitten" because of its shape, faces a strip of Canadian territory across Lake Huron — the only point where Canada lies directly south of the United States. Mackinaw City stands at the northern end of the end of the "mitten," at the Straits of Mackinac.

Michigan's origins go back to the 1600s, when the French were settling this area. The state's nickname derives from the great number of wolverines caught by French fur trappers. In 1641, Father Jacques Marquette, the French missionary and explorer, founded a trading post and mission, the first permanent European settlement in Michigan, at Sault Ste. Marie. At this time, Michigan was still home to the Ojibwa (Chippewa), Ottawa, and Menominee tribes.

The largest city is Detroit, founded by Antoine de la Mothe, Sieur de Cadillac, in 1701. The city is famous today for its automobile industry. This is where most American cars and other motor vehicles are designed and manufactured. Various other industries, including defense, space, and food processing are located around Detroit. The Upper Peninsula is a beautiful land of lakes and pine forests. Sawmills and fishing provide some industry, but this area is foremost a vacation spot, attracting campers, canoeists, and hikers. The climate in this region is very cold in winter. The state is truly a "Water Wonderland," as Michigan license plates proclaim. It has 3,121 miles (5,023 km) of shoreline, longer than the Atlantic coast from Maine to Florida. It also has 11,000 inland lakes and thousands of waterways.

DETROIT
The 73-story Renaissance Center complex in downtown Detroit reflects the city's revived fortunes. The covered walkway is part of a nearly 3-mile (5-km) long "People Mover." The city also boasts a symphony orchestra, and the original home of the black "soul" music label Motown Records.

White pine

Robin

STATE SYMBOLS

Apple blossom

AVIATOR HERO
Pioneer aviator Charles Lindbergh stands beside the "Spirit of St. Louis" which he helped design, and which took him on the first non-stop solo flight across the Atlantic on May 20–21,1927. Lindbergh was born in Detroit in 1902, and spent his early years as a "barnstormer", performing aerial tricks and daredevil stunts. He returned from his trailblazing flight to a ticker-tape welcome in New York City, followed by a 48-city tour with his plane.

LAKE MICHIGAN
Lake Michigan is the only one of the five Great Lakes to lie entirely within the boundaries of the United States. Apart from Michigan, the other states that surround it are Illinois, Indiana, and Wisconsin. It is the third-largest of the Great Lakes, measuring 321 miles (517 km) from north to south, and 118 miles (190 km) from east to west. It is also the fifth-largest freshwater lake in the world. The lake joins Lake Huron at the Straits of Mackinac, where Michigan's two peninsulas nearly meet. The most important of Michigan's ports on the lake is Escanaba. Iron ore leaves Escanaba bound for the steel mills of Gary, Indiana. Fisheries are important, but there are serious pollution problems at the southern tip of the lake.

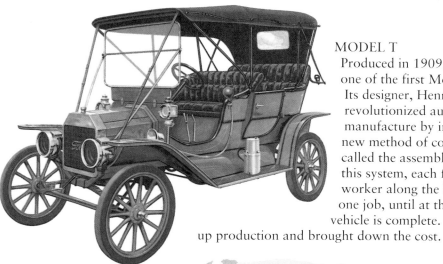

MODEL T
Produced in 1909, this was one of the first Model T Fords. Its designer, Henry Ford, revolutionized automobile manufacture by introducing a new method of construction called the assembly line. With this system, each factory worker along the line performs one job, until at the end, the vehicle is complete. This speeded up production and brought down the cost.

FARMLAND
There are around 90,000 farms in Michigan, most of them in the southern half of the Lower Peninsula. Although the state is not known primarily for its agricultural output, it does produce corn, winter wheat, soybeans, honey, and flowers. The Saginaw Valley produces dry beans and sugar beets. There is a wide fruit-producing belt along Lake Michigan and other farm products include milk, poultry, and pigs.

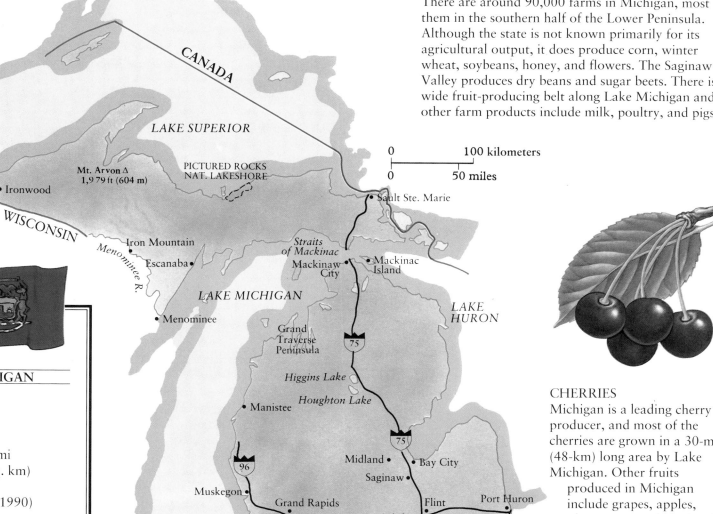

0 —— 100 kilometers
0 —— 50 miles

CHERRIES
Michigan is a leading cherry producer, and most of the cherries are grown in a 30-mile (48-km) long area by Lake Michigan. Other fruits produced in Michigan include grapes, apples, peaches, pears, and blueberries. The blossoms attract bees, whose honey is another important Michigan product. More cultivated sour cherries come from Michigan than from any other state. Many sour cherries are used to make alcoholic drinks called liqueurs.

MICHIGAN

Capital
Lansing
Area
58,527 sq. mi
(151,585 sq. km)
Population
9,295,297 (1990)
Largest cities
Detroit (1,027,974),
Grand Rapids (189,126)
Statehood
January 26, 1837
Rank: 26th
Principal rivers
Grand, Muskegan
Highest point
Mount Arvon,
1,979 feet (604 m)
Motto
*Si Quaeris Peninsulam
Amoenam Circumspice*
(If You Seek a Pleasant
Peninsula, Look About You)
Song
"Michigan, my Michigan"

MINNESOTA

The northernmost state in the United States, apart from Alaska, Minnesota is also known as the North Star State. Car license plates proclaim "10,000 lakes," but in fact there are over 15,000, and the scenic beauty of the state attracts visitors from all over the nation. Minnesota is also one of the Great Lakes states, with its northeastern border on Lake Superior. Here, at the busy port of Duluth, timber, grain, iron ore, and industrial goods are shipped to other states along the 2,342-mile (3,768-km) route, via the lakes and the St. Lawrence Seaway, to the Atlantic. In the southeast of the state the twin cities of Minneapolis–St. Paul straddle the Mississippi River and dominate the surrounding region. Minneapolis is one of the most important manufacturing cities in the United States. Among the goods produced are food products and electronic equipment. Grain from the Midwest is stored here, too, before being shipped to other destinations. St. Paul is the state capital. Southern Minnesota is largely prairie land, where farms produce soybeans, corn, and sugar beets. Wheat and other grains contribute to the state's wealth, as does the dairy industry. Other Minnesota products include pulp and paper, and iron ore.

French Canadians were the first settlers in the region. They encountered Native American tribes, including Chippewa and Sioux. The land east of the Mississippi came under U.S. control in 1783, and that to the west was part of the Louisiana Purchase of 1803. Later an influx of Norwegians, Swedes, and Danes settled in Minnesota to work in the mining and timber trades. In the 1900s black Americans came to work in the factories, followed by Poles, Germans, Hispanics, and Asians.

BALD EAGLE
Much of northern Minnesota consists of vast tracts of forests sprinkled with clear-blue lakes. Such a wilderness attracts the bald eagle, the national symbol. Although rare, it favors the western Great Lakes region because of its fish diet.

HIGH-TECH INDUSTRY
Minnesota is a leading state in the computer industry, and some of the world's foremost manufacturers have high-tech plants in Minneapolis-St. Paul. In this picture, workers are examining a magnified computer circuit board.

Pink and white lady's slipper

Red (Norway) pine

STATE SYMBOLS

Common loon

MINNEAPOLIS
New glass office towers and hotels, tree-lined plazas, fountains, and even enclosed pedestrian skyways (an alternative to the normally frozen winter walkways) all indicate that Minneapolis is a thriving city. Much of its wealth comes from business, including computers, but also from its long-standing milling industries. Household names such as Pillsbury, Nabisco, and General Mills have their mills here.

MINNESOTA

Capital
St. Paul
Area
84,402 sq. mi
(218,601 sq. km)
Population
4,375,099 (1990)
Largest cities
Minneapolis
(368,383),
St. Paul (272,235),
Duluth (85,493)
Statehood
May 11, 1858
Rank: 32nd
Principal rivers
Minnesota, Mississippi
Highest point
Eagle Mountain,
2,301 feet (702 m)
Motto
L'Etoile du Nord
(The Star of the North)
Song
"Hail! Minnesota"

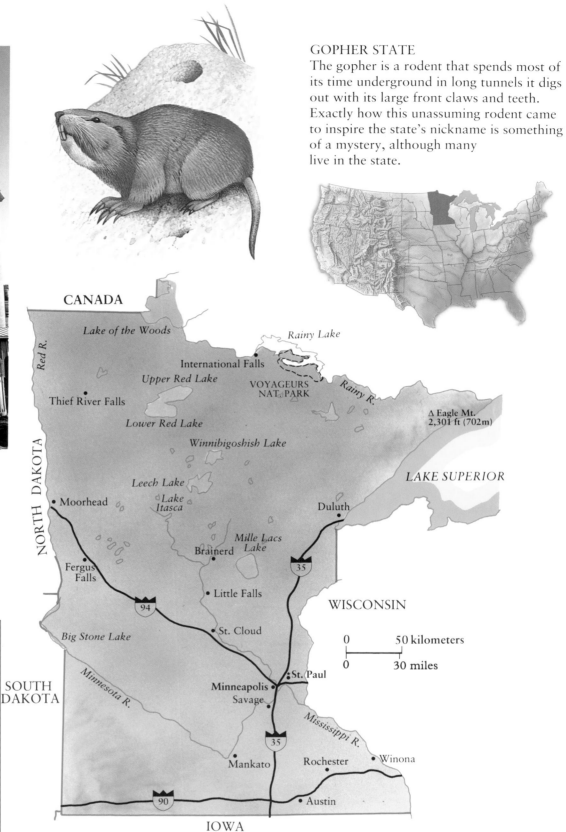

GOPHER STATE
The gopher is a rodent that spends most of its time underground in long tunnels it digs out with its large front claws and teeth. Exactly how this unassuming rodent came to inspire the state's nickname is something of a mystery, although many live in the state.

Map labels

CANADA

Lake of the Woods

Rainy Lake

International Falls

Upper Red Lake

VOYAGEURS NAT. PARK

Red R.

Thief River Falls

Rainy R.

Lower Red Lake

Winnibigoshish Lake

Δ Eagle Mt. 2,301 ft (702m)

LAKE SUPERIOR

Leech Lake

Lake Itasca

NORTH DAKOTA

Moorhead

Duluth

Mille Lacs Lake

Brainerd

Fergus Falls

35

Little Falls

WISCONSIN

94

0   50 kilometers

Big Stone Lake

St. Cloud

0   30 miles

SOUTH DAKOTA

Minnesota R.

St. Paul

Minneapolis

Savage

Mississippi R.

35

Mankato

Rochester

Winona

90

Austin

IOWA

GRAIN STORAGE STATE
In this dramatic photograph, a grain truck is tilted to empty its load into the elevator. Several of America's — indeed some of the world's — largest grain and cereal companies are based in Minnesota. Minneapolis has grain storage for over 120 million bushels — the highest in the United States.

HARVESTING RICE
Two Native Americans of the Chippewa tribe knock ripe wild rice into their canoe at Leech Lake, in the north of the state. The rice is sold commercially. The Chippewas were among the first tribes in the region, though in prehistoric times Minnesota was inhabited by mound builders. The Chippewas hunted, fished, and gathered wild rice for food. Today they work in many professions. Some live on reservations in Minnesota and North Dakota.

LAKE ITASCA
Lake Itasca is the source of the mighty Mississippi River. It lies in Lake Itasca State Park. Minnesota's thousands of lakes attract canoeists, fishermen, and those who enjoy nature. Animal life includes moose, wolves, beavers, red foxes, and bears. Acres of forest and wildflowers contribute to the state's natural beauty. The rock formations along the lake shores serve as a useful source of information for geologists.

MISSISSIPPI

A "Deep South" state, Mississippi has 88 miles (142 km) of coastline along the Gulf of Mexico between Louisiana and Alabama. The Mississippi River, from which the state takes its name, forms the western border with Louisiana and Arkansas. Along the northern border is Tennessee. Most of the land is flat plains — the highest point in the state is only 806 feet (246 m) high — with rich soil for agriculture. The climate is warm and humid in summer, with mild and short winters. Such soil and climate traditionally encouraged a farming economy, with cotton as the main crop. In the pre-Civil War days, slaves worked on huge cotton plantations owned by wealthy whites. These were the antebellum days, when cotton was "king" and white plantation owners enjoyed the spoils of a slave-run economy in their grand balconied mansions. Poorer whites, however, had to compete in a backward rural environment, and many were no better off educationally, socially, or economically than the black slaves. Mississippi became the second state to leave the Union before the Civil War, and Jefferson Davis, himself a Mississippi resident, became President of the Confederate States of America. During the war, from 1861 to 1865, many battles were fought in the state, causing much damage, particularly at Vicksburg. After the war, the state reverted to being a poor agrarian and racially segregated region. Cotton, along with timber, remained the chief business, and industrialization did not begin until the 1930s with the discovery of oil and the growth of factories turning out textiles, transportation equipment, and electrical goods. The civil rights movement in the 1960s began, finally, to achieve equal rights for black Americans. Today they account for over 35 percent of the total population — higher than any other state.

MISSISSIPPI OIL
An oil platform at Pascagoula, the chief port of Mississippi. The state ranks in the top ten as an oil producer, and oil, along with natural gas, is drilled from a number of offshore wells in the Gulf of Mexico.

STATE SYMBOLS

Mockingbird

Magnolia flower

Magnolia tree

GRACIOUS HOUSES
Antebellum (pre-Civil War) mansions that belonged to the cotton plantation owners are well preserved in Mississippi, and attract tourists from all over the country. Natchez, sitting atop a high bluff by the Mississippi River, has many such houses dating from the early- to mid-1800s, including Melrose House shown here. Vicksburg, which saw one of the key battles of the Civil War, also has fine examples. The names of the houses — Auburn, Rosedale, Shadowlawn, Rosalie — recall a sedate, tranquil time, at least for the plantation owners. Life for the slaves was often very harsh.

COTTON ECONOMY
Cotton plantations, such as the one depicted in this illustration, were the centers of rural life in the Southern states before the Civil War. The scene looks idyllic, with a paddle steamer gliding down the Mississippi River in the background and the plantation owners in their fine clothes. Much of the South's wealth before the Civil War came from cotton, which was exported as a raw material for new textile mills both in other states and overseas. Money from cotton helped finance the Confederacy at the beginning of the war.

MISSISSIPPI

Capital
  Jackson
Area
  47,689 sq. mi
  (123,515 sq. km)
Population
  2,573,216 (1990)
Largest cities
  Jackson (196,637),
  Biloxi (46,319)
Statehood
  December 10, 1817
  Rank: 20th
Principal rivers
  Mississippi, Yazoo, Pearl
Highest point
  Woodall Mountain,
  806 feet (246 m)
Motto
  Virtute et Armis
  (By Valor and Arms)
Song
  "Go, Mississippi!"

QUEEN OF THE DELTA
The delta is the fertile flood plain between the Mississippi and Yazoo rivers. Here, from the early 1800s onward, paddle steamers, such as this fine example, the *Delta Queen*, transported passengers and goods along the Mississippi River. Today such paddle steamboats carry mainly tourists on the stretch from Natchez to Vicksburg. Forests of hardwood trees and steep bluffs line many parts of the Mississippi River. Along its course, the river has cut off areas of land as it meanders, creating small islands.

CATCHING CATFISH
Three men wade deep to pull in their nets full of Mississippi catfish. These larger versions of the catfish family are also farmed in lakes and streams and are much prized for their taste. They are bottom-dwellers and use feelers to search for food as they move along. Varieties in the Mississippi River Valley are the channel catfish, the blue catfish, and the yellow catfish. Farther south, at the port of Biloxi, there is a thriving shrimp fleet, which is blessed annually at a special ceremony on the water. Fishing remains an important industry for Mississippi, and catches include menhaden, red snappers, oysters, and carp.

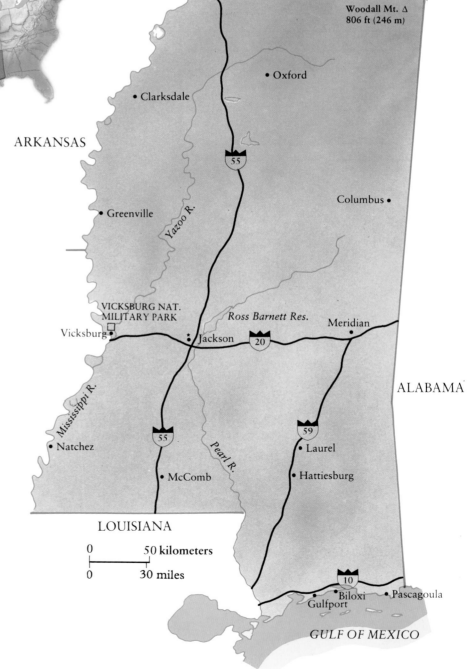

TENNESSEE

Woodall Mt. △
806 ft (246 m)

• Oxford

• Clarksdale

ARKANSAS

• Greenville

Yazoo R.

Columbus •

VICKSBURG NAT.
MILITARY PARK

Ross Barnett Res.

Meridian •

Vicksburg •   • Jackson

ALABAMA

Mississippi R.

Pearl R.

• Laurel

• Natchez

• McComb

• Hattiesburg

LOUISIANA

0   50 kilometers
0   30 miles

Biloxi
Gulfport   • Pascagoula

GULF OF MEXICO

MISSOURI

Near the geographical center of the continental United States lies the Midwest state of Missouri. It shares borders with eight other states — Arkansas, Iowa, Illinois, Kansas, Kentucky, Nebraska, Oklahoma, and Tennessee. Missouri's history and economy have been shaped by the two great rivers that flow through the state — the Mississippi and the Missouri. The Mississippi forms the eastern border, while the Missouri forms the northwestern border down to Kansas City, where it swings inland across the state. It eventually joins the Mississippi just north of St. Louis.

Missouri is a prosperous state, in both agriculture and industry. Its factories make more manufactured goods than all other states excluding Texas and California. Aircraft, spacecraft, automobiles, leather goods, chemicals, and beer are among the diverse products. Anheuser-Busch, based in St. Louis, is the largest brewery in the world. The contribution to the state economy from manufacturing is worth double that of farming, timber, and mining combined. Livestock, especially cattle, and dairy products are very important, and the chief crops are corn, wheat, soybeans, and cotton. Missouri is the number-one lead producer, and second in zinc mining. Lime and cement are also produced. Even when the French first founded Ste.Genevieve, the oldest town in the state, around 1735, lead mining was already established. The United States acquired Missouri from the French in 1803 as part of the Louisiana Purchase. The invention of the steamboat, and use of the Mississippi and Missouri rivers as major transport routes made the state a center of commerce early in its history. Missouri joined the Union as a slave state in 1821, under the terms of what was called the Missouri Compromise. By this treaty, Maine also became a state — a free state — to keep the number of slave and free states equal. However, Missouri remained loyal to the Union during the Civil War.

STATE SYMBOLS

Bluebird

Flowering dogwood

Hawthorn

MARK TWAIN
Author Mark Twain grew up in Hannibal, a town he made famous in *The Adventures of Tom Sawyer* and many other works. The town has a Mark Twain museum, including the two-room cabin, originally situated in a nearby settlement, in which he was born, as Samuel Clemens, in 1835.

OZARK PLATEAU
These springs form part of the Ozark National Park. The Ozark Plateau covers the southern part of Missouri. This region is one of hilly forests and low mountains. It is also an area of thousands of cold, moist, and damp caves. Such caves once provided shelter for outlaws such as Jesse James and the Dalton Gang. The Ozark Mountain region is also famous for its special brand of Ozark country music and its chain of lakes which are popular with anglers. Table Rock Lake lies at the center of this chain; the other lakes include Bull Shoals, and Taneycomo.

JESSE JAMES
The James gang, led by Jesse James and his brother Frank, staged about 25 violent bank and train robberies in Missouri. Innocent railroad workers were often killed. The famous outlaw was born in Missouri in1847. He fought on the Southern side during the Civil War with a band of guerillas known as Quantrill's Raiders. After the war James and his gang started their robberies, hiding from the law in Missouri's many caves. After a reward was offered to catch him dead or alive, James was shot by one of his own gang in 1882.

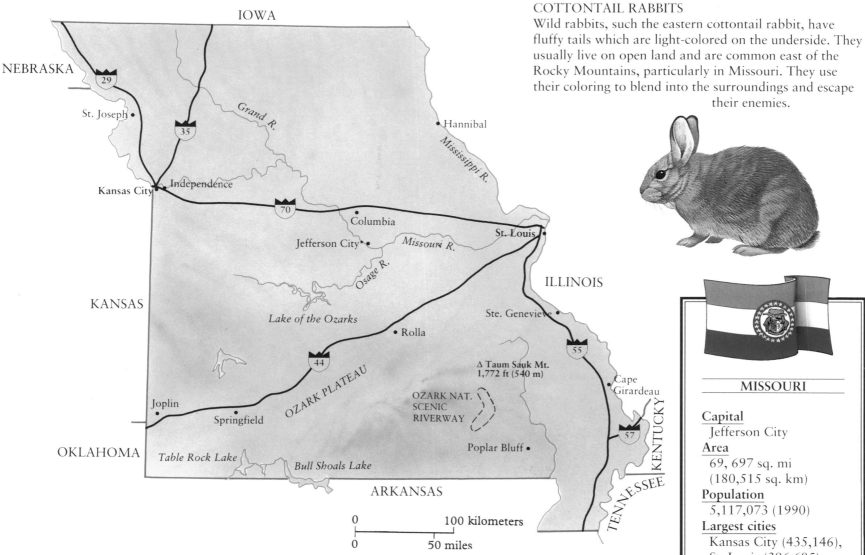

COTTONTAIL RABBITS

Wild rabbits, such the eastern cottontail rabbit, have fluffy tails which are light-colored on the underside. They usually live on open land and are common east of the Rocky Mountains, particularly in Missouri. They use their coloring to blend into the surroundings and escape their enemies.

MISSOURI	
Capital	
Jefferson City	
Area	
69, 697 sq. mi	
(180,515 sq. km)	
Population	
5,117,073 (1990)	
Largest cities	
Kansas City (435,146),	
St. Louis (396,685)	
Statehood	
August 10, 1821	
Rank: 24th	
Principal rivers	
Missouri, Mississippi	
Highest point	
Taum Sauk Mountain,	
1,772 feet (540 m)	
Motto	
Salus Populi Suprema	
Lex Esto (The Welfare	
of the People Shall Be	
the Supreme Law)	
Song	
"Missouri Waltz"	

ST. LOUIS — GATEWAY TO THE WEST

The gleaming curve of Gateway Arch forms a backdrop to the modern skyline of St. Louis. The arch itself is stainless steel and was built in 1965. Its height of 630 feet (192 m) is unmatched by any other national monument. The arch commemorates the thousands of pioneers who passed through St. Louis on their way west, and at its base there is a Museum of Westward Expansion. St. Louis is the most important inland port along the Mississippi, and is 10 miles (16 km) south of where the Missouri River meets the Mississippi.

PLYING ITS TRADE

A giant barge carries its cargo on the Mississippi River which forms Missouri's eastern border. Most freight on the Mississippi is carried in large barges such as this one. Agricultural products, coal, and steel make up most of the cargo.

MONTANA

Montana is the fourth largest state in the country, but has fewer than one million people — only five per square mile. The name of this northwestern state comes from the Spanish word for "mountainous," although 75 percent of the land is flat or gently rolling Great Plains. It is in western Montana, lying in the Rocky Mountains, that the land rises to between 6,500 and 13,000 feet (2,000 and 4,000m) above sea level. To the north, Montana shares its border with three Canadian provinces — Saskatchewan, Alberta, and British Columbia. In the southwest of the state, the Missouri River begins its great journey in the Rocky Mountains, and then runs eastward across the state. The Yellowstone River is also an important river in the state. Both rivers supply vitally-needed water to humans, cattle, and crops. Montana has a continental climate, which means that it has very cold winters and hot summers. Until Alaska joined the Union, Montana was the coldest state.

It is on the Plains that vast herds of cattle and sheep — among the largest numbers in the country — graze. Montana is also a producer of barley, wheat, and sugar beets, and there is a large timber industry. But, as its nickname of "Treasure State" suggests, Montana is a land rich in natural minerals, particularly gold, silver, copper, and coal.

The United States acquired most of Montana in the Louisiana Purchase of 1803, and soon after, Lewis and Clark explored the region. Fur traders started visiting the area, and the Native American tribes that lived there began to resist the growing influx of white settlers prospecting for gold. The Battle of the Little Bighorn, or Custer's Last Stand, took place in Montana in 1876, between the U.S. cavalry and a coalition of Native American tribes. The opening of the Northern Pacific Railroad in 1883, and a major silver discovery in 1886, near Butte, led to more settlers arriving and to the state joining the Union in 1889.

SPARSELY POPULATED LAND
Livingston is situated in the south-central part of the state. It lies on the Yellowstone River in Gallatin National Forest, which adjoins Yellowstone National Park. Livingston itself is typical of the small, sparsely-populated towns of the state, with its quiet main street. At nearby Bozeman, the dinosaur exhibit at Montana State University draws many tourists.

MONTANA

Capital
Helena
Area
147,046 sq. mi
(380,849 sq. km)
Population
799,065 (1990)
Largest cities
Billings (81,151),
Great Falls (55,097),
Missoula (42,918)
Statehood
November 8, 1889
Rank: 41st
Principal rivers
Missouri, Yellowstone,
Clark Fork
Highest point
Granite Peak,
12,799 feet (3,904m)
Motto
Oro y plata
(Gold and silver)
Song
"Montana"

BIGHORN CANYON
Spreading across the Montana-Wyoming border, Bighorn Canyon provides spectacular scenic and historic sites. Nearby Yellowtail Dam has created a 71-mile (114-km) reservoir which is popular with anglers and water-sports enthusiasts. Tourism is important to the state's economy, with hunters, fishermen, and campers vacationing in Montana's many parks. The southwest boundary of the state borders Yellowstone National Park, while the northern border with Canada includes Glacier National Park — with over 60 glaciers.

STATE SYMBOLS

Ponderosa pine

Western meadowlark

Bitterroot

SCATTERED FARMS

Like islands in a sea of checkered wheatfields, farmhouses stand out on the flat Great Plains of Montana. Immense fields of winter wheat are typical of the eastern part of the state. Agriculture serves as the state's greatest source of income, and Montana ranks in the nation's top ten in the production of wheat and barley. Livestock, particularly cattle, sheep, and pigs, accounts for 50 percent of agricultural income. There are over 2.25 million cattle in the state.

THE SWIFT PRONGHORN

The pronghorn lives in open grassland, typically on the high Great Plains of Montana. It is one of North America's fastest mammals, and can travel at speeds of up to 44 miles per hour (70km/h), which enables it to outrun wolves and coyotes. It is often called the American antelope, although it is not a true antelope.

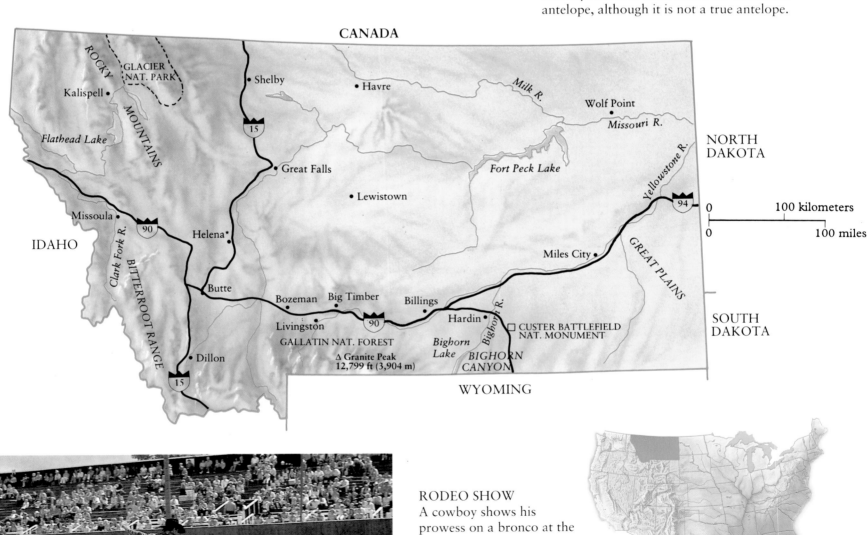

CANADA

GLACIER NAT. PARK

ROCKY MOUNTAINS

Kalispell

Shelby

Havre

Milk R.

Wolf Point

Missouri R.

NORTH DAKOTA

Flathead Lake

Great Falls

Fort Peck Lake

Yellowstone R.

94

0   100 kilometers

Lewistown

0   100 miles

Missoula

Clark Fork R.

90

Helena

Miles City

GREAT PLAINS

IDAHO

BITTERROOT RANGE

Butte

Bozeman   Big Timber   Billings

SOUTH DAKOTA

Livingston   90   Hardin

Bighorn R.

CUSTER BATTLEFIELD NAT. MONUMENT

Dillon

GALLATIN NAT. FOREST
Δ Granite Peak
12,799 ft (3,904 m)

Bighorn Lake

BIGHORN CANYON

15

WYOMING

RODEO SHOW

A cowboy shows his prowess on a bronco at the Big Timber Rodeo. Rodeo is a form of entertainment featuring cowboys and cowgirls who demonstrate their riding and roping skills. It developed from the cowboy cattle-herding days in the western United States from the mid-1860s to the late 1880s. The main events at rodeos are bareback bronco riding, saddle bronco riding, bull riding, calf roping, and steer wrestling (or bulldogging). With a strong cowboy tradition in Montana, it is not surprising that there are many rodeo shows in the state.

NEBRASKA

Nebraska, in the heart of the Great Plains, is one of the great farming states of the nation, and its nickname of "Cornhusker State" refers to its most valuable crop. Most of Nebraska is prairie land, but near its western border with Colorado and Wyoming, the elevation reaches one mile high. Nebraska has very cold winters and hot summers. Blizzards and windstorms often hit the state, as do droughts. Farmers get their water supply from the Missouri River in the east, which separates the state from Iowa and Missouri, and from the Platte River, which runs west–east across the state. Most industry is related to farming: Omaha, the largest city, is one of the country's leading meat-packing centers. Factories in the state also process grain into breakfast food. Other manufactured items include machinery, electrical goods, metal products, and transportation equipment. Natural minerals in the state include petroleum and natural gas. Construction industries use large amounts of sand and gravel from the Platte Valley, and limestone is used to make cement.

Before the Louisiana Purchase of 1803, the area had been visited by French and Spanish trappers and fur traders in the 1700s. Lewis and Clark also passed through in 1804–1806 on their famous expedition through the Louisiana Territory. The first permanent settlement was at Bellevue, near Omaha, in 1823. The Homestead Act of 1862 encouraged many Civil War veterans to move to Nebraska with the promise of cheap land. Pioneers, prospectors, and cowboys passed through Nebraska following the Oregon Trail, or the routes used by the Mormons or by Lewis and Clark. They were helped on their journeys by such landmarks as Chimney Rock and the 800-foot (244-m) high Scotts Bluff, on the state's western edge. Pony Express riders also used these landmarks as route guides. Buffalo Bill held his Wild West show in North Platte, and Jesse James and his gang roamed the plains. The transcontinental railroad, which came through in 1863, also helped to open up the region. Nebraska is unique in having a one-house state legislature (all other states have an upper and a lower house). The Capitol where it meets has a 350-foot (107-m) high tower.

STATE SYMBOLS

Cottonwood

Western meadowlark

Goldenrod

LINCOLN

Founded in 1859, Lincoln was originally named Lancaster, but was renamed in honor of the Civil War president, Abraham Lincoln. The Sheldon Art Gallery, which contains some fine paintings, the Folsom Children's Zoo, and the University of Nebraska are located in Lincoln.

NEBRASKA

Capital
Lincoln

Area
77,355 sq. mi
(200,349 sq. km)

Population
1,578,385 (1990)

Largest cities
Omaha (355,795),
Lincoln (191,792),
Grand Island (39,386)

Statehood
March 1, 1867
Rank: 37th

Principal rivers
Platte, Nebraska,
Republican

Highest point
Johnson Township,
5,426 feet (1,654m)

Motto
Equality Before the Law

Song
"Beautiful Nebraska"

BUFFALO BILL'S HOME

Near North Platte, in the west-central part of Nebraska, is Buffalo Bill Ranch State Historical Park. Frontier scout and cowboy–showman William F. "Buffalo Bill" Cody lived in this house while he put together his Wild West rodeos. So popular were his shows that one "Old Glory Blow-Out" held at North Platte in 1872 attracted 1,000 contestants. Bill started a traveling Wild West show, which opened in Omaha in 1883. These shows popularized his and other cowboys' skills across the United States and overseas.

THE SIOUX

The Sioux are a Great Plains tribe, and Nebraska was one of their hunting grounds (along with Minnesota and South Dakota). During the 1860s and 1870s the Sioux fought against European settlers who were trying to make homesteads in these states. There was constant fighting between the U.S. Army and Sioux warriors led by chiefs Crazy Horse, Red Cloud, and Sitting Bull. The Sioux used their skills as horsemen to outmaneuver the heavily armed U.S. troops. They were highly effective at the Battle of the Little Bighorn in Montana. These modern day Sioux (above) are dressed in their ceremonial costumes.

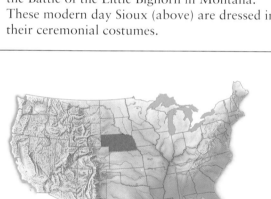

A GREAT FARMING STATE

Nebraska is one of the most important farming states in the nation. It ranks behind only Texas and Iowa in the number of cattle and calves — 6 million — raised in the state each year. It also raises over 4 million hogs and over 2 million turkeys. Much of the cattle grazing takes place in the Sand Hills region of western Nebraska, and cowboys patrolling their vast herds in this area are a common sight. The output of its 50,000 farms equals the value of the state's industries, timber, and mining combined. After corn, the most valuable crops are hay, oats, wheat, sorghum, soybeans, and sugar beets.

UNELECTED PRESIDENT

The 38th President of the United States, Gerald R. Ford, was born in Omaha on July 14, 1913. He was the only president not elected to the office. He was appointed, not elected, as vice-president, and took over the presidency from Richard Nixon who resigned in 1973.

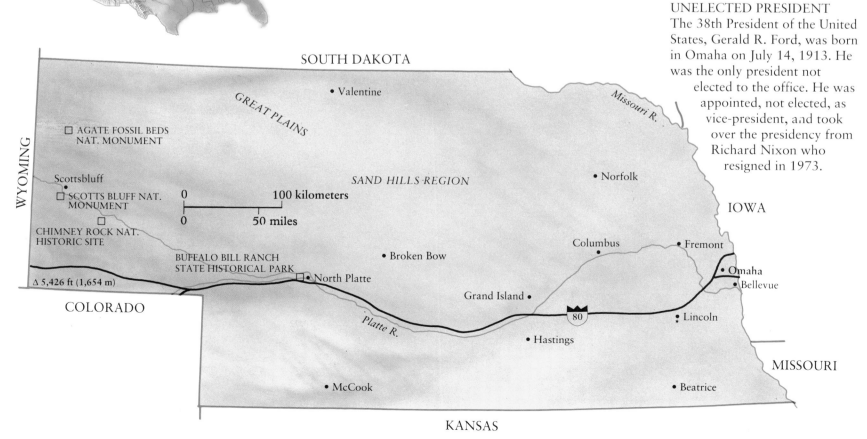

SOUTH DAKOTA

GREAT PLAINS

• Valentine

☐ AGATE FOSSIL BEDS NAT. MONUMENT

WYOMING

Scottsbluff
☐ SCOTTS BLUFF NAT. MONUMENT

☐

CHIMNEY ROCK NAT. HISTORIC SITE

SAND HILLS REGION

Missouri R.

• Norfolk

IOWA

0   100 kilometers

0   50 miles

BUFFALO BILL RANCH STATE HISTORICAL PARK

△ 5,426 ft (1,654 m)

COLORADO

☐ • North Platte

• Broken Bow

Columbus

80

Grand Island •

Platte R.

• Hastings

• Fremont

• Omaha
• Bellevue

• Lincoln

MISSOURI

• McCook

• Beatrice

KANSAS

NEVADA

If it were not for the lure of gold, silver, and gambling, Nevada might have remained a vast, mainly uninhabited land of rugged mountains, arid desert, buttes, and mesas. Nevada is the driest and one of the hottest states in the Union. The land receives an average of only 4 inches (10 cm) of rain and snow in a year — compared to neighboring Oregon's annual 60 inches (152 cm) along its coast. Other states that border this Rocky Mountain state are Idaho, to the north; Utah, to the east; Arizona, at its southern tip across the Colorado River and the famous Hoover Dam; and California, to the west. The boundary with California runs at such an angle that Carson City, the state capital, actually lies farther west than Los Angeles. Some 85 percent of the land is owned by the federal government — much of it used for the testing of weapons.

Paiute Indians were the first inhabitants and so unwelcoming was the terrain that it was one of the last parts of the West to be explored — dying of thirst was a real danger for early explorers. Mormons were the first white settlers in this inhospitable terrain; they established the first settlement, Mormon Station (now Genoa), in 1849. The discovery of gold and silver brought thousands of prospectors to establish mining towns, including Virginia City. Many such places are now deserted "ghost towns." Gold and silver remain important sources of income, and Nevada leads all states in the production of these metals.

However, one-third of the jobs in the state come from the gambling and entertainment resorts of Las Vegas and Reno. Tourism is the state's primary source of income, and the main industry is the manufacture of gambling equipment, followed by chemicals, aerospace products, and irrigation equipment. There is some farming in the state, with just over half a million cattle. Alfalfa and potatoes are the main crops. The timber industry, produces wood pulp from piñon and juniper trees.

LAKE TAHOE
Lying on the Nevada-California border, Lake Tahoe has a 72-mile (116-km) shoreline of public beaches and parks, as well as resorts and gambling casinos. It is the largest mountain lake on the North American continent. The lake lies 6,226 feet (1,899 m) above sea level, surrounded by snow-capped mountains.

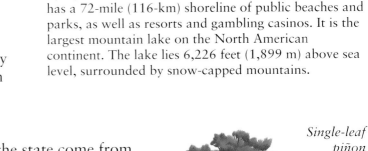

Single-leaf piñon

Mountain bluebird

STATE SYMBOLS

Sagebrush

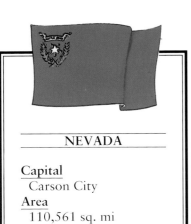

NEVADA

Capital
Carson City
Area
110,561 sq. mi
(286,353 sq. km)
Population
1,201,833 (1990)
Largest cities
Las Vegas (258,295),
Reno (133,850),
Paradise (124,682)
Statehood
October 31, 1864
Rank: 36th
Principal rivers
Columbia,
Humboldt
Highest point
Boundary Peak,
13,140 feet (4,007m)
Motto
All for Our Country
Song
"Home Means
Nevada"

CITY OF NEON
Las Vegas beckons tourists, with its giant neon signs, to the many casinos, hotels, entertainment centers — and even to places where you can get instant marriages and instant divorces. Early Indians called the Basketmakers inhabited the region from 300 B.C. to A.D. 1150. Spanish explorers came in 1776 and founded Las Vegas, naming it after the Spanish words for "the meadows." Until this century it was a farming community. Gambling was made legal in 1931 and this provided the impetus to develop a city in the middle of nowhere, and out of nothing. Las Vegas is now the state's largest city and also boasts the largest resort hotel in the world.

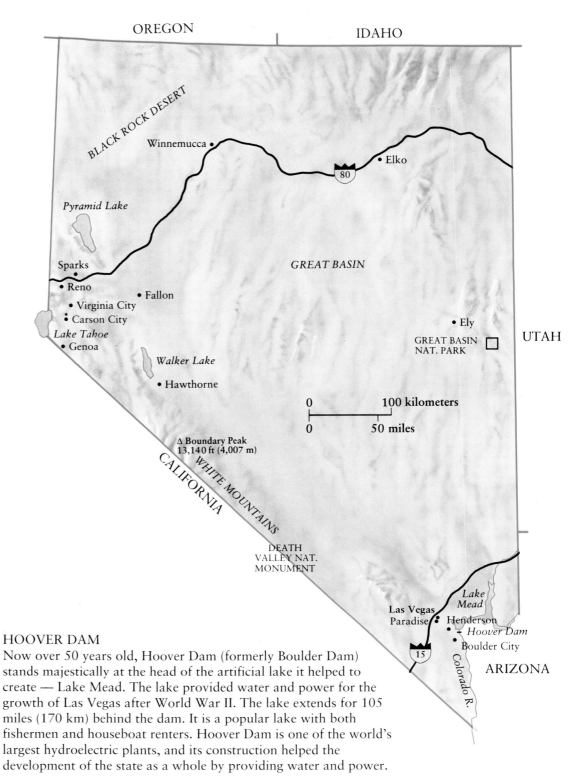

BRISTLECONE PINES
North of Death Valley, which runs across the Nevada–California border, stand bristlecone pines. They are high up — 13,000 feet (4,000 m) — in the White Mountains, and accessible only in summer. They are reputed to be the oldest trees on earth, and some have been dated back over 4,500 years. Probably the oldest one of all, named Methuselah, is almost 4,700 years old. They are twisted by the wind, and their few bristles, or needles, stay on the tree for up to 30 years.

HOOVER DAM
Now over 50 years old, Hoover Dam (formerly Boulder Dam) stands majestically at the head of the artificial lake it helped to create — Lake Mead. The lake provided water and power for the growth of Las Vegas after World War II. The lake extends for 105 miles (170 km) behind the dam. It is a popular lake with both fishermen and houseboat renters. Hoover Dam is one of the world's largest hydroelectric plants, and its construction helped the development of the state as a whole by providing water and power.

RATTLESNAKES
Among the most poisonous of snakes, rattlesnakes live in dry western regions, such as Nevada's deserts. The snake often gives a warning before it strikes, by lifting its tail and shaking the rattle on its end. Its venom is injected by its sharp fangs, and can quickly paralyze, and eventually kill, its prey.

NEW HAMPSHIRE

Located in the northeastern corner of the United States, New Hampshire is the third-largest of the six New England states. It was the first colony to declare independence from England, and every four years it is the first state to hold U.S. presidential primary elections. This makes the state the focus of media attention as the candidates come to national prominence — for many of them it is the first and only time. No candidate in recent history has lost this primary and gone on to be president.

New Hampshire has a narrow 18-mile (29-km) stretch of Atlantic coastline, and its greatest width is only a little over 90 miles (150 km). From north to south it measures 180 miles (290 km) but narrows to a northern border with Canada of just 15 miles (24 km) across. In the north are the White Mountains, which have the rock outcroppings that have given New Hampshire its nickname of the "Granite State." Mount Washington, the highest peak in the Northeast, at 6,288 feet (1,917 m), is also located there. This peak is one of the windiest places on the planet; the highest known wind speeds have been recorded there. New Hampshire's most famous landmark is a rock formation, the Old Man of the Mountains, also called the Great Stone Face. It is located in the Franconia Range of the White Mountains and stands 40 feet (12 m) high. The Connecticut River runs along most of the state's western border with Vermont. Over 80 percent of the land is covered by forest — white pine, hemlock, oak, and birch — which yields lumber, wood pulp, and paper products. Most of New Hampshire's people and industries are in the southern part of the state. Tourism and forestry are the major industries, followed by the manufacture of machinery, electrical products, plastics, and metal products. The four largest cities are all located in this region, and all once had textile mills. Many of the newer manufacturers have moved there from the nearby Boston area because New Hampshire has lower taxes.

Abnaki Indians, the first-known Native Americans in New Hampshire, were driven out by English settlers, who settled there in 1623. In the 1800s New Hampshire was noted for its textile mills, and many French Canadians came to work these mills at that time. Today, there are still more French Canadians in New Hampshire than in any other state.

White birch

STATE SYMBOLS

Purple finch

Purple lilac

NEW HAMPSHIRE

Capital
Concord
Area
9,279 sq. mi
(24,033 sq. km)
Population
1,109,252 (1990)
Largest cities
Manchester (99,567),
Nashua (79,662),
Concord (36,006)
Statehood
June 21, 1788
Rank: 9th
Principal rivers
Connecticut,
Merrimack,
Androscoggin
Highest point
Mt. Washington,
6,288 feet (1,917m)
Motto
Live Free or Die
Song
"Old New Hampshire"

FRANKLIN PIERCE
The 14th president of the United States, Franklin Pierce, was born in New Hampshire and served in the New Hampshire legislature from 1829 to 1833. He was elected president in 1852, at a time when conflict between North and South over slavery was deepening. He was a compromise candidate who was trusted by the South, even though he was a Northerner.

RURAL MOUNTAIN LAND
A covered wooden pedestrian bridge spans a thickly wooded river valley in Franconia Notch State Park in New Hampshire. Notches are long wooded gaps, or deep valleys and land forms that separate the mountains. Franconia Notch is a famous landmark in the state. Another is Profile Mountain, which bears the rock formation known as the Great Stone Face. The White Mountains, in which these landmarks are located, cover the northern third of the state.

PORTSMOUTH

Lying at the north of New Hampshire's short stretch of Atlantic coastline, Portsmouth is the fifth-largest city in the state. The port developed during the Industrial Revolution of the 1800s with its textile mills, woodworking, shoemaking, and clothing manufacture. In the 1950s the textile mills gave way to factories and other firms developing high technology. The Portsmouth naval shipyard at Kittery builds and repairs submarines for the U.S. Navy.

FALL IN NEW HAMPSHIRE

Traditional colonial architecture, set in tranquil and beautiful countryside, is one of the reasons why tourism has become New Hampshire's main industry. Come fall, visitors from other parts of the United States crowd the state to witness the panorama of colors on the trees. The leaf colors are at their finest from September to mid-October. At this time the weather is invigorating and quite chilly. Snow abounds in the mountains during the winter months.

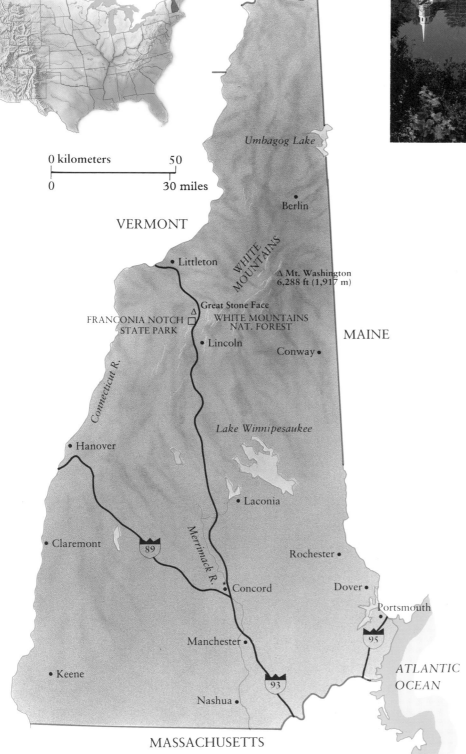

MT. WASHINGTON RAILWAY

This famous cog railway takes vacationers to the 6,288-foot (1,917-m) summit of New Hampshire's highest mountain. The 3½-mile (5.5-km) line has been in operation since the 1860s. It offers superb views of the surrounding tree-covered White Mountains. A network of trails spread out from Mt. Washington, attracting hikers, campers, skiers, fishermen, and hunters.

NEW JERSEY

A small state in area, New Jersey is hemmed in between two of the largest urban complexes in the United States — New York City and Philadelphia. Many people drive through or commute between these cities, hardly seeing New Jersey at all. However, they are missing a state of surprising variety. It is surrounded by water on all sides except for the 50-mile (80-km) border with New York to the north. New Jersey has a stretch of Atlantic coastline that runs for 130 miles (209 km). To the northeast are the Hudson River and Lower New York Bay. The Delaware River serves as the state's western border with Pennsylvania, flowing south into Delaware Bay.

Farms in the central and southwestern parts of the state give New Jersey its nickname of "Garden State" — a somewhat surprising title, as the entire population is classified as living in metropolitan areas. But market gardening is a major business, and the land has rich soil, ideal for growing crops such as potatoes, peaches, cranberries, and blueberries, as well as tomatoes, corn, hay, and soybeans. New Jersey ranks in the top ten for manufacturing; among its products are pharmaceutical drugs, chemicals, and petroleum products. The state has witnessed many famous scientific inventions, including Thomas Edison's invention of the electric light and the phonograph. Edison set up the nation's first research laboratory in New Jersey in 1876.

A thriving fishing industry brings in catches of menhaden, clams, and swordfish. The first residents in the state were Delaware Indians, and the first Native American Reservation in the country was set up for them in 1758, by the English settlers who had arrived there in 1664. The English took over from earlier Dutch and Swedish settlers.

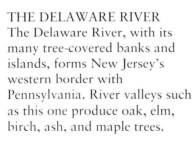

Eastern goldfinch

Purple violet
STATE SYMBOLS

ON THE BOARDWALK
Atlantic City is a well-known resort town on the southeast coast of New Jersey, and is especially famous for its 4½-mile (7.2-km) boardwalk. The first boardwalk was built in 1870 and was only 8 feet (2m) wide. The modern version has amusement piers which jut out from it, adding to the carnival atmosphere with vendors, exhibits, shows, and food outlets. Gambling is also legal.

Red oak

THE DELAWARE RIVER
The Delaware River, with its many tree-covered banks and islands, forms New Jersey's western border with Pennsylvania. River valleys such as this one produce oak, elm, birch, ash, and maple trees.

A STADIUM FOR GIANTS
The Meadowlands, only a few miles from New York City, offers a unique sports and entertainment stadium. It opened at East Rutherford in 1976 and remains one of the most modern sports complexes in the world. The New York Giants professional football team plays there, despite its location in New Jersey. Other attractions at the stadium include basketball and harness racing.

HIGH-TECH LABORATORY
A worker inspects power circuits at the Bell Telephone Laboratories in New Jersey. The laboratory researches and develops telephones and other telecommunications. Started at the beginning of the 1900s, the laboratory constructed the pioneer electrical digital computer, and some of its staff have won Nobel Prizes for their research.

OPOSSUM
Opossum are most common in the central and eastern parts of the country, such as New Jersey. They have more teeth than any other North American mammal — 50 in all — and use their long tails to hang from tree branches.

BATSTO MILL
This gristmill — a mill for grinding grain into flour — is found at Batsto, a partially restored village in southeastern New Jersey that dates from colonial times. The community produced cannonballs for George Washington's troops during the Revolutionary War. Other attractions at the village include a blacksmith's shop, a general store, and a glassware exhibition.

NEW JERSEY

Capital
Trenton
Area
7,787 sq. mi
(20,168 sq. km)
Population
7,730,188 (1990)
Largest cities
Newark (275,221),
Jersey City (228,537),
Paterson (140,891),
Elizabeth (110,002)
Statehood
December 18, 1787
Rank: 3rd
Principal rivers
Delaware, Hudson
Highest point
High Point,
1,803 feet (550 m)
Motto
Liberty and Prosperity
Song
None

Δ High Point
1,803 ft (550 m)

NEW YORK

Paterson
Clifton
MORRISTOWN NAT.
HISTORICAL PARK
West Orange
East Rutherford
Newark
Jersey City
Elizabeth

PENNSYLVANIA

Raritan R.

Delaware R.

Princeton
Long Branch

0   50 kilometers
0   30 miles

Trenton

Willingboro

Camden

Mullica R.

Vineland
Gt. Egg Harbor R.
ATLANTIC OCEAN

Maurice R.

DELAWARE

Atlantic City

Delaware Bay

Hudson R.

PRINCETON UNIVERSITY
Students sit outside the attractive Princeton clock tower of this famous university, founded in 1746. It is one of the oldest and finest universities in the country. The campus is in the town of Princeton itself. The great physicist Albert Einstein worked there when he first arrived in the United States. The town of Princeton is also home of Princeton Battlefield, scene of a decisive American victory in 1777 by General George Washington in the Revolutionary War.

NEW MEXICO

A land of beautiful deserts, mesas, mountains, canyons, caves, and buttes, New Mexico is justly named the "Land of Enchantment." Its history goes back thousands of years and embraces several different cultures: those of cliff-dwelling Native Americans, whose ancient pueblos can still be seen, and whose descendants live there today; of Spanish colonists, who established a capital at Santa Fe in 1609 (about the same time as the first British settlements on the Atlantic coast); of Mexicans, who owned the territory between 1821 and 1848; and finally, of white Americans, who began moving into the territory in the mid-1800s. In 1945 New Mexico came to the world's attention as the site of the first testing of the atomic bomb.

The Rocky Mountains enter the state along its northern border with Colorado. Arizona is to the west and to the south lie Mexico and part of Texas, which also takes up most of the eastern border. New Mexico has very little surface water — less than any other state — so irrigation for both livestock and crops is vital. Crops include cotton, hay, onions, wheat, pecans, and sorghum. Much of the land is grazed by cattle and sheep. Most of the state's wealth comes from minerals — oil and natural gas. New Mexico is the leading state in the mining of potash and uranium. Copper, silver, iron, and lead are also mined.

It was the prospect of silver and gold that first lured the Spanish explorer Francisco Coronado to the area in 1540 and that led to the forming of a colony in 1598. The same metals brought another wave of settlers to work the mines in the 1800s. When Mexico gained independence from Spain in 1821, New Mexico became part of that country. Following the Mexican War of 1846–1848, the territory was acquired by the United States, but it was disputed until 1912 when New Mexico became a state. The state has one of the largest Mexican and Spanish-American populations in the United States.

CHURCHES MADE OF MUD
San Geronimo Church, in Taos, displays the typical pueblo architecture of adobe walls, enclosed patios, buttressed corners, and portals. New Mexico's generally dry and sunny climate has ensured the survival of such buildings for centuries. In 1671, Spanish settlers discovered an Indian pueblo that had existed in Taos from around A.D. 1000. There was much trade of grain, pottery, and jewelry between the Spanish, Pueblo Indians, and other Native Americans who traveled from across the mountains.

Yucca

Piñon

STATE SYMBOLS   *Roadrunner*

RIO GRANDE GORGE
Near the Spanish-Indian village of Taos lies this spectacular gorge, carved by the Rio Grande. The elevation is 2,500 feet (763 m), and the gorge is often covered with snow in winter. Farther upriver, Glen Canyon Dam backs up the water of the Colorado River to make Lake Powell — the second-largest manmade lake in the United States. Extensions of Lake Powell run into countless canyons, creating steep, dark red walls with deep blue waters.

NEW MEXICO

Capital
Santa Fe
Area
121,593 sq. mi
(314,926 sq. km)
Population
1,515,069 (1990)
Largest cities
Albuquerque (384,736),
Las Cruces (62,126),
Santa Fe (55,589)
Statehood
January 6, 1912
Rank: 47th
Principal rivers
Rio Grande, Gila,
Pecos
Highest point
Wheeler Peak,
13,161 feet (4,014 m)
Motto
Crescit Eundo
(It Grows As It Goes)
Song
"O, Fair New Mexico"

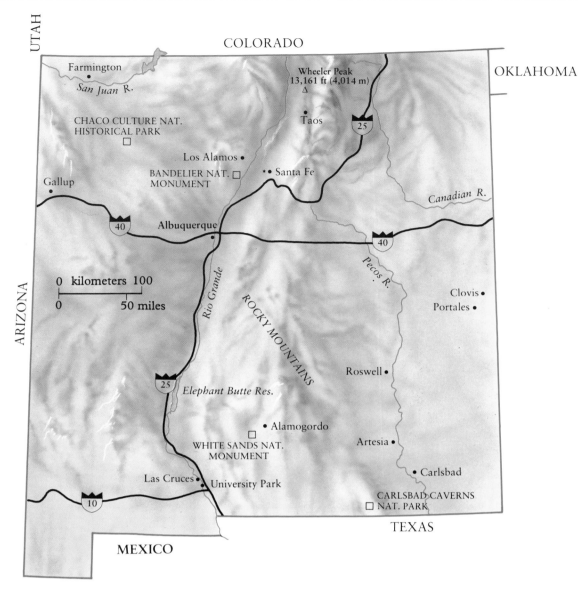

HOPI SUN GOD
Hopi kachinas (spirit followers) wear colorful face masks representing a variety of gods, spirits, and clouds, including the sun god, Tawa Kachina, shown here. The Hopi, are the most western group of Pueblo Indians. Most live in northeastern Arizona, but some make their home along New Mexico's border with Arizona. Most of them are farmers and shepherds.

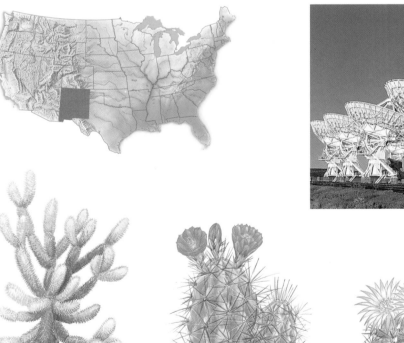

TRACKING THE STARS
The Very Large Array radio telescope contains 27 radio dishes spread over 13 miles (21km), to the north of White Sands Missile Range, where military missiles are tested. New Mexico is a state in which nature's destructive — as well as beneficial — forces have been exploited. Many people in the state are employed in atomic, space, military, and other scientific research, and this contributes to the economy. It was on July 16, 1945, that the world's first atomic bomb was tested just north of Alamogordo. Within a month two other bombs were dropped on Hiroshima and Nagasaki, in Japan, ending World War II.

Teddybear cholla

Claret cup cactus

Cushion cactus

Beavertail cactus

Peyote

DESERT BLOOM
Desert flowers blooming overnight after a sudden thunderstorm are reminders that New Mexico is indeed a state of enchantment. Cacti survive the dry climate of New Mexico by storing up large amounts of water in their stems. The thick, waxy skin keeps the water in, instead of allowing it to evaporate as in other plants. The sharp needles protect the plants against animals and birds. For a very brief period every year, the cacti produce stunning white, red, pink, and yellow flowers. These in turn attract many insects, including butterflies.

NEW YORK

The second most populous state in the country, New York falls into two distinct parts: New York City — whose metropolitan area extends into New Jersey and Connecticut — and "upstate" New York. New York lies in the Northeast, with many natural boundaries, including Lake Ontario, Lake Erie, Lake Champlain, the Niagara River and Falls, the Atlantic Ocean, and the St. Lawrence and Hudson rivers. Ships ply the St. Lawrence Seaway, and the extensive canal system, linking the state to the Midwest and to Canada.

The state has varied and beautiful countryside. To the north lie the Adirondack Mountains, with peaks over 5,000 feet (1,500 m) high. The large Allegheny Plateau has much farmland devoted to fruit and dairy products. It also includes the aptly named Finger Lakes. The plateau almost completely surrounds the Catskill Mountains, with their many lakes and resorts. New York's climate is continental, which brings hot summers with cold, snowy winters. In the summer, people flock to the beaches, particularly those on Long Island. Long Island extends eastward from the mouth of the Hudson River for about 120 miles (193 km). Other key attractions include the spectacular Niagara Falls, the Thousand Islands (where the St. Lawrence River meets Lake Ontario, most of which is in Canada), and of course Manhattan, the center of New York City. The city contains the famous Empire State Building (named for the state itself), the Statue of Liberty, the World Trade Center towers, and many other famous sights, and is the nerve center of the nation's banking, finance, trade, communications, publishing, arts, and fashion. Tourists come from all over the world to enjoy its concert halls, museums, art galleries, theaters, clubs, and restaurants.

The Italian navigator Giovanni da Verrazano (after whom a bridge linking Staten Island to Brooklyn in New York City is named) first visited the region in 1524. The Dutch established a settlement there in 1621, and in 1625, Governor Peter Minuit purchased Manhattan Island from local Indians for $24 worth of trinkets. The British took control in 1664 and named it New York after the Duke of York, later King James II of England.

Sugar maple

STATE SYMBOLS

Rose

Bluebird

LADY WITH THE TORCH
The Statue of Liberty, on Liberty Island in New York Harbor, was erected in 1883. It was a gift from France, and it became the first landmark sighted by poor and oppressed immigrants coming in by ship across the Atlantic — a symbol of their entry into a new and free land. The framework is iron, and it is covered in copper. The lady stands 151 feet (46 m) tall, on a pedestal 154 feet (47 m) high.

ADIRONDACK COUNTRYSIDE
Autumn colors surround the Black River in the Adirondack Mountains, in northeastern New York. The 100 or so mountains that make up the Adirondack range include New York State's highest, Mt. Marcy, at 5,344 feet (1,630 m). Over 200 lakes, including long Lake George, lie within this mountain region, which covers 5,000 sq. miles (13,000 sq. km). Sadly, there is evidence of acid rain on many lakes. The Adirondacks are covered with spruce, hemlock, and pine forests, and were named by Samuel de Champlain in 1609, after a local tribe.

NEW DEAL PRESIDENT
Franklin Delano Roosevelt was born in New York on January 30, 1882, and became the 32nd U.S. president in 1933. The economic Depression was at its worst, but his "New Deal" presidency overhauled the banking system, gave aid to farmers, and financed many public projects. He was helped with many of his duties by his wife Eleanor.

NIAGARA FALLS

Niagara Falls straddles the border between New York State and Ontario, in Canada. In fact there are two falls, the American falls, 176 feet (54 m) high and 1,000 feet (305 m) wide, and the (Canadian) Horseshoe Falls, which are 167 feet (51 m) high and 2,600 feet (792 m) wide. A famous excursion boat, *Maid of the Mist*, takes tourists right to the base of the American Falls.

NEW YORK	
Capital	Albany
Area	49,108 sq. mi (127,190 sq. km)
Population	17,990,455 (1990)
Largest cities	New York City (7,322,564), Buffalo (328,123), Rochester (231,636)
Statehood	July 26, 1788 Rank: 11th
Principal rivers	Hudson, Mohawk, St. Lawrence
Highest point	Mt. Marcy, 5,344 feet (1,630 m)
Motto	*Excelsior* (Ever Upward)
Song	"I Love New York"

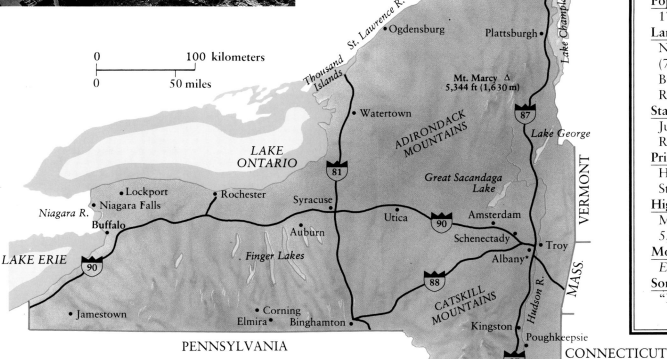

CENTRAL PARK

Wintertime in Central Park, at the heart of Manhattan, brings skaters and walkers seeking a peaceful refuge from the New York City's hustle and bustle. The park has been the setting for large concerts, including one attended by 750,000 people to hear New York singer-songwriter Paul Simon in 1991. It is surrounded by elegant 19th-century hotels and apartment blocks.

BROOKLYN BRIDGE

Opened in 1883, the Brooklyn Bridge was hailed, in its time, as the eighth wonder of the world. This suspension bridge crosses the East River, linking the borough of Brooklyn with Manhattan. The other three boroughs of the city are Queens, the Bronx, and Richmond (Staten Island). The bridge is 1,595 feet (486 m) long and was the first to use steel for cable wire. It was the longest in the world until the Firth of Forth rail bridge in Scotland was completed in 1890. There is a broad promenade above the roadway — a distinctive feature — and the bridge takes both automobile and passenger traffic.

NORTH CAROLINA

The southern state of North Carolina has a long history and a richly-varied landscape. Its coastline includes many inlets and islands — one of them the site of the first English colony in North America — enclosed by a long chain of sandbars, called the Outer Banks. The shifting sands of these banks are notoriously dangerous for ships, hundreds of which have foundered on them — especially off Cape Hatteras, the "Graveyard of the Atlantic." Also on the Outer Banks is Kitty Hawk, where the Wright brothers ushered in the age of powered flight. West of the islands is the coastal plain. The average elevation here is less than 20 feet (6 m). Tobacco, North Carolina's most important crop, is grown here. Much of the early work was done by slaves from Africa who were freed after the Civil War. Other crops include soybeans, corn, and peanuts. Farther west is the Piedmont, a rolling plateau that contains the state's chief population and industrial centers. Charlotte, the largest city, is located here. Despite being a rural state, North Carolina leads all states in textiles and furniture production. In fact, it is one of the leading industrial states in the nation. High technology products are made at Research Triangle Park, a research center founded in 1959 by three universities.

The Piedmont also has most of the state's thriving poultry raising industry. West of the Piedmont the land rises to the Blue Ridge Mountains, and beyond that are the higher Great Smoky Mountains — the highest mountains in the eastern half of the nation. Roanoke Island, inside the Outer Banks, is the site where, between 1585 and 1591, the British attempted to establish their first colony in North America. In 1587 Sir Walter Raleigh sent 117 colonists, under Governor John White, to settle there. Relations with Native Americans were difficult, and the colonists received little help from their sponsors in England. When a ship bearing fresh supplies finally arrived in 1591, the whole colony had vanished. To this day, no one knows what happened to the "Lost Colony." But before they disappeared, they baptized the first child born of English parents in the New World, White's granddaughter, Virginia Dare. The first permanent settlement was established later in 1653.

STATE SYMBOLS

Pine

Cardinal

Flowering dogwood

TOBACCO
Clusters of star-shaped blossoms identify the tobacco plant. North Carolina produces about two-fifths of the U.S. output. Native Americans smoked tobacco as a sacred herb before the first colonists began growing it.

THE FIRST FLIGHT
A memorial atop a sand dune commemorates the point from which Orville and Wilbur Wright successfully accomplished the first sustained flight in a craft heavier than air. On December 17, 1903, their "Flyer I" took off at Kitty Hawk. The flight lasted 12 seconds, and that was enough to signal the age of the airplane. Only a few people witnessed this historic event. Orville piloted the first short flight. His brother made a second, longer flight, lasting nearly a minute. In 1908 Orville made a one-hour flight. The original planes are now in the National Air and Space Museum in Washington, D.C.

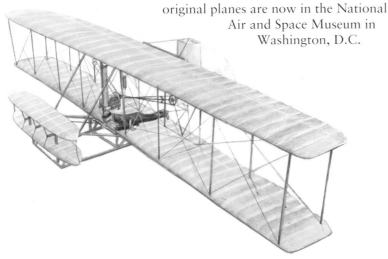

BLUE RIDGE MOUNTAINS
The Blue Ridge Mountains are the major range in North Carolina. The mountain region covers some 6,000 sq. mi (15,539 sq. km). The temperatures here are cool, and the land is covered mainly with hardwood forests. South of the range is the Piedmont plateau, half of which is covered with timber. It also contains the state's cities and industry.

NORTH CAROLINA

Capital
Raleigh

Area
52,669 sq. mi
(136,413 sq. km)

Population
6,628,637 (1990)

Largest cities
Charlotte (395,934),
Raleigh (207,951),
Greensboro (183,521)

Statehood
November 21, 1789
Rank: 12th

Principal rivers
Roanoke, Yadkin,
Neuse

Highest point
Mt. Mitchell,
6,684 feet (2,038 m)

Motto
Esse Quam Videri (To
Be Rather Than to Seem)

Song
"The Old North State"

CHARLOTTE

Charlotte, the state's largest city, is one of the fastest growing towns in the nation. It is a center for textiles, machinery, metal, and food processing. It was settled in about 1750, and named after Queen Charlotte, wife of George III of England. In the early 1800s a gold mint was located there and it was the center of U.S. gold production until the Gold Rush of 1849. During the Civil War, it was an important Confederate naval yard. Presidents Andrew Jackson and James Polk were both born nearby and educated in the city.

BLACK BEAR

The black bear is a good climber and lives in forests all over the United States. So North Carolina, with its large areas of forest-covered land, is an ideal environment for this mammal. Bears are the largest meat-eating animals (carnivores) on the continent, and the smallest of them — the black bear — is the most common species.

POINT HARBOR

This attractive harbor lies on Albemarle Sound, at the tip of a small, sharp peninsula where the Intracoastal Waterway meets the Pasquotank River and flows into the Atlantic Ocean. Just east, across a short stretch of water, is Kitty Hawk, the site of the Wright brothers' momentous experiment in powered flight. Their achievement is commemorated by the Wright Brothers National Memorial. Point Harbor is also at the north end of the Cape Hatteras National Seashore. There are many long sandy beaches, nature trails, and waterfowl refuges located here.

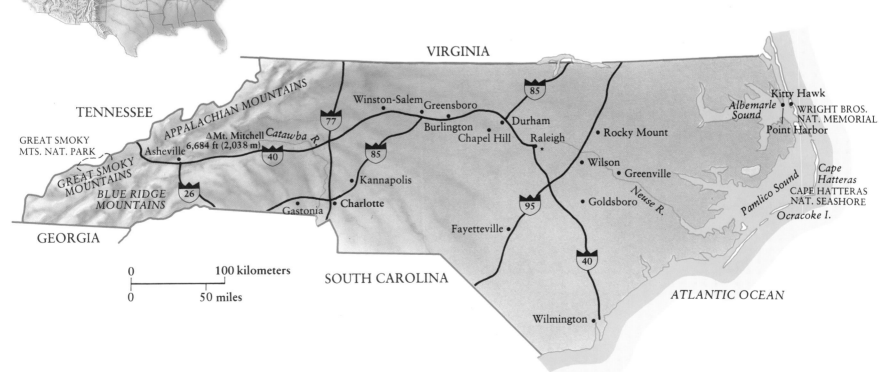

NORTH DAKOTA

The Great Plains state of North Dakota lies at the center of continental North America. In fact, the geographical center is in Pierce County, 6 miles (10 km) west of Balta, at latitude 48° 10'N, longitude 100° 10' W. North Dakota's economy is based heavily on farming; the land consisting typically of enormous farms on treeless prairies. The climate is extreme in the state, with summer temperatures reaching as high as 120° F (50° C) and bitterly cold winters falling as low as − 60° F (− 50° C). The sharp contrasts in climate and the nature of the land may account for the small population of North Dakota — the fourth-smallest in the United States.

The state rises slowly from the prairie of the east to the high plateau of the west. The Red River forms its eastern border. The Missouri River enters from the west and runs through the center of the state. Eastern North Dakota is especially good for farming despite a short growing season with little rain. The average farm is an enormous 1,000 acres (405 hectares in size). The state has substantial deposits of oil and coal, but has the least manufacturing of any state. Farm machinery and food products are the main manufactured items.

The western part of the state is too dry for crops, but beef cattle graze there on pastureland. The so-called Badlands are located here, consisting of strange land formations and contours formed by the erosion of soft rock. Directly on the North Dakota border between Canada and the United States lies the International Peace Garden. The land was donated by the two countries as a tribute to over 150 years of peaceful relations.

The first Europeans to visit North Dakota were French fur trappers and traders traveling from Canada in the 1700s. Sioux Indians were already established there, and "Dakota" means an alliance of Sioux tribes. Bad relations with the Sioux hindered early white settlement, but the first railroad in the 1870s attracted many more settlers.

BADLANDS
Strange rock formations, the result of millions of years of erosion by wind and water, dominate the skyline in North Dakota's Badlands, in the southwest. Table-like mesas and buttes — steep hills standing alone on the plain — are the result of major erosion caused by a large, fast-flowing river which dried up millions of years ago. The name "Badlands" was given to the region by pioneers who found the land difficult to cross. White Butte, situated in the Badlands, is the highest point in the state.

NORTH DAKOTA

Capital
Bismarck
Area
70,702 sq. mi
(183,118 sq. km)
Population
638,800 (1990)
Largest cities
Fargo (77,111),
Grand Forks (49,425)
Statehood
November 2, 1889
Rank: 39th
Principal rivers
Missouri, Sheyenne,
Little Missouri
Highest point
White Butte,
3,506 ft (1,069m)
Motto
Liberty and Union,
Now and Forever,
One and Inseparable
Song
"North Dakota Hymn"

ROOSEVELT NATIONAL MEMORIAL PARK
In 1884, Theodore Roosevelt retired temporarily from politics and came to North Dakota to hunt buffalo. He stayed to start up two ranches at Elkhorn and Maltese Cross. The Roosevelt National Memorial Park, one of more than 40 in the state, is a wilderness with coyotes, Rocky Mountain sheep, and buffalo amid buttes and hills.

STATE SYMBOLS

American elm

Wild prairie rose

Western meadowlark

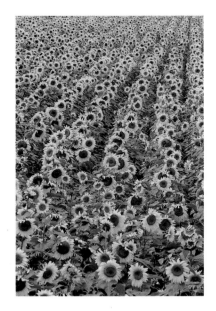

SUNFLOWERS
The common sunflower is cultivated in North Dakota for its oil, which is used as cooking or salad oil. The remainder of the seed can be made into cattle-cake and food for poultry. Sunflowers can grow as tall as 13 feet (4 m).

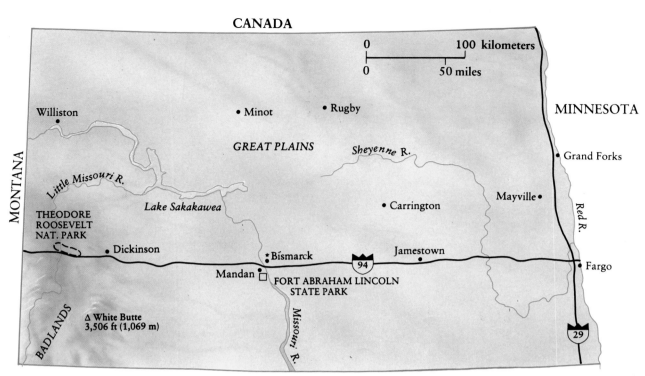

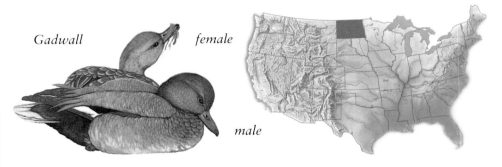

Gadwall *female*

male

WATERFOWL
Every summer ducks, such as gadwalls and mallards, and geese migrate to North Dakota to breed in the lakes, marshes and grain fields. More waterfowl hatch in North Dakota than in any other state. Another animal native to the state is the flickertail squirrel, from which the state gets its nickname.

Mallard

male

female

A WHEAT STATE
A typical view of North Dakota's farming-dominated land, where giant grain elevators dot the horizon beyond bales of hay ready for collection. Over 90 percent of the land is cropland or pasture. Agriculture far exceeds manufacturing in the state. Wheat is the chief crop; North Dakota is second only to Kansas in wheat production. Other important crops are barley, rye, and oats. Durum wheat, used in making pasta, is grown in the driest areas, where it is particularly suited to the soil and climate. Beef and dairy cattle are also raised in North Dakota. The richest farmlands are in the Red River Valley and on the Great Plains, which stretch from the northwest to the south-central part of the state. North Dakota is the chief flax-growing state.

SACAGAWEA
When Meriwether Lewis and William Clark set out to explore the lands bought by the United States in the Louisiana Purchase of 1803, they had a Shoshone Indian woman to guide them westward. Her name was Sacagawea, which means "Bird Woman," and she was from North Dakota. She was married to a French Canadian trapper, who acted as an interpreter. Carrying her baby on her back, Sacagawea was influential in appeasing potentially hostile Indian tribes with messages of peace.

OHIO

Ohio lies at the eastern edge of the Midwestern region. It has more industries, and is more urban than almost any other state. The basis of its economy has traditionally come from what are called "smokestack industries," such as steel mills, automobile factories, tires and other rubber products, as well as petroleum, plastics, and chemicals. Several of these industries were set up in the 1850s and 1860s. Ohio is also an important agricultural state, and in the 1850s ranked first in farming. Despite its heavy industrial base, Ohio still has 60 percent of its land given over to farming. The chief crops are corn, hay, and winter wheat, but tobacco is grown in the south, and there are fruit farms along the banks of the Ohio River. Much of the corn is fed to cattle raised in the state.

Some of Ohio's farmers belong to the Amish sect, who still practice a mainly non-mechanized form of farming. They have lived in the state since the 1800s. The eastern part of the state is the most industrialized, but the major cities are fairly well scattered — from Cleveland in the northeast, to Columbus, in the center of the state, and Cincinnati in the southwest corner. Dayton, also in the west, is an aviation center, with the Wright–Patterson Air Force Base located nearby. The Wright Brothers first experimented with kites, gliders, and flying machines at this field. The U.S. Air Force Museum, at the base, is one of the largest in the world. The first cash register was also made in Dayton, by an inventor named James Ritty. Akron, in the northeast, is an important center for rubber manufacture; some of the most famous tire companies in the world are based there. The first rubber plant was started in Akron in 1879, and the arrival of the automobile, toward the end of the century, created an enormous demand for pneumatic tires. Columbus, the capital, is the fastest-growing city in the state. Its limestone state capitol building remains one of the finest examples of Greek Revival architecture. Presidents who were born or lived at some time in Ohio include William McKinley, Rutherford B. Hayes, William Henry Harrison, Benjamin Harrison, Ulysses S. Grant, James A. Garfield, and William Howard Taft.

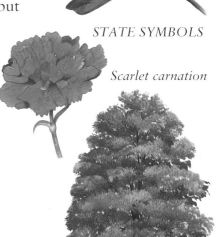

Cardinal

STATE SYMBOLS

Scarlet carnation

Buckeye

BASEBALL

The Cincinnati Reds are Ohio's National League baseball team. They play at the impressive Riverside Stadium, built in 1970 with artificial grass. Baseball quickly gained popularity after the rules of the game were established in 1845. The National League, founded in 1876, was the first professional league. The American League followed in 1900. In 1990 the Reds won the World Series.

CLEVELAND

Cleveland stands at the mouth of the Cuyahoga River on Lake Erie. It was founded by Moses Cleveland in 1796, when Ohio was part of the Northwest Territory. The city suffered a severe debt problem in the 1970s, but has come back as a busy commercial center with improved streets and bridges. The city is also an art center, with the world-famous Cleveland Orchestra, the Cleveland Museum of Art, and the Natural History Museum. Cleveland lies close to deposits of coal and iron, which makes it an important iron and steel producer.

OHIO	
Capital	
Columbus	
Area	
41,330 sq. mi	
(107,045 sq. km)	
Population	
10,847,115 (1990)	
Largest cities	
Columbus (632, 910),	
Cleveland (505,616),	
Cincinnati (364,040)	
Statehood	
March 1, 1803	
Rank: 17th	
Principal rivers	
Ohio, Cuyahoga,	
Miami, Sandusky	
Highest point	
Campbell Hill,	
1, 550 feet (472 m)	
Motto	
With God, All Things	
are Possible	
Song	
"Beautiful Ohio"	

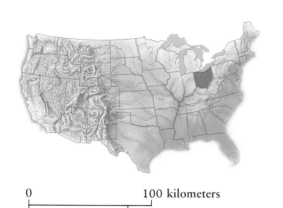

0   100 kilometers
0   50 miles

CANADA

LAKE ERIE

MICHIGAN

PERRY'S VICTORY INT.
PEACE MEMORIAL
• Toledo
90
• Sandusky   **Cleveland**
80
90
71   80   Niles •
Findlay •   76
Akron   • Youngstown
• Canton

Lima •   Mansfield •
• Wapakoneta
*Grand
Lake*   75
△ Campbell Hill
1,550 ft (472 m)   71
Springfield   • Newark   77
Columbus   70
Zanesville •
• Dayton
Lancaster •
Middletown •
MOUND CITY GROUP
NAT. MONUMENT
□
• Chillicothe
Cincinnati •   • Hillsboro

Portsmouth •

KENTUCKY

INDIANA

PENNSYLVANIA

Ohio R.

WEST VIRGINIA

CINCINNATI
A nighttime river scene in Cincinnati. The city straddles the Ohio River close to the border with Kentucky. Also located here is the home of the Taft family, including the 27th U.S. president, William Howard Taft. Cincinnati has a big meat industry, linked to transport on the Ohio River.

AUTOMOBILE INDUSTRY
The manufacturing of transportation equipment is the largest industry in Ohio. The state produces more buses and trucks than any other state, as well as a high percentage of automobiles. Overall, Ohio ranks third in the United States in manufacturing.

BURIAL MOUNDS
Serpent Mound, near Hillsboro, is shaped like a giant snake. These burial mounds were built by some of Ohio's earliest inhabitants. They put well-crafted items such as copper breastplates, tools, shells, carved pipes, and ornaments made of grizzly bear teeth in the mounds.

FIRST MAN ON THE MOON
Neil Armstrong uttered the memorable phrase, "That's one small step for a man, one giant leap for mankind," as he became the first man to set foot on the moon on July 20, 1969. He was born in Ohio and began his career as a Navy pilot. Armstrong joined the space program as an astronaut in 1962. His initial mission, in 1966, in Gemini 8, involved the first docking in space. With Edwin Aldrin and Michael Collins, he made the Apollo 11 moon mission.

OKLAHOMA

The outline of Oklahoma looks rather like a clenched fist with a pointing finger. The finger, or panhandle (a strip of land that stretches out from the main region like the handle of a pan), extends for 175 miles (282 km) to the New Mexico border. Most of the land is gently rolling prairie but has suffered badly from soil erosion, and in the 1930s terrible windstorms blew much of the topsoil away, creating the famous "Dust Bowl." A great deal of land has since been reclaimed. In the dry areas of the state, the main crops are wheat and hay; in the humid zones, sorghum, peanuts, and cotton are grown. Like Texas, to the south, Oklahoma derives most of its farm income from cattle ranching, and is also an oil state. Its manufacturing industries produce machinery, plastics, and rubber goods.

A state rich in Native American, cowboy, and homesteader history, Oklahoma's name comes from a Choctaw Indian word meaning "red people," and the land was originally the home of many Native American tribes, including the Comanche and Osage. The "Five Civilized Tribes" — Cherokee, Chickasaw, Choctaw, Creek, and Seminole — were forced by the government to settle there, and the territory was designated Indian land. But on April 22, 1889, the territory was opened up for settlement by homesteaders. Thousands of people on horseback and in covered wagons lined up to begin, literally, a race to stake land claims and to build homesteads. By nightfall some 10,000 settlers had poured onto the land. Some, however, had "jumped the gun" and staked land illegally. They were called "sooners," from which the state gets its nickname. Despite this land seizure, the state today holds the highest Native American population of any state — about 250,000.

STATE SYMBOLS

Redbud

Mistletoe

Scissor-tailored flycatcher

COTTON PICKING
Oklahoma's Red River region, in the southeast corner of the state, forms part of the fertile lowlands that stretch south, eventually reaching the Gulf of Mexico, and which provide fertile ground for growing cotton. Grains, dairy products, and livestock outrank cotton in terms of income, but this staple crop is important to the state's economy. The southeast corner, where the cotton is grown, has a humid climate and has been called "Little Dixie."

COWBOY COMEDIAN
Actor and cowboy comedian Will Rogers was a famous Oklahoman entertainer of the early 1900s. Born in 1879, he developed a stage act, combining rope tricks with humorous comments about events of the time. In 1926 President Coolidge sent Rogers overseas as an "ambassador of good will."

TOWERING TULSA
In the 1920s, Tulsa had more millionaires than any other city in the United States. Their wealth came chiefly from oil and from other minerals extracted around the city. This metallic-looking building is the City of Faith Medical Center, which rises 60 stories. Beside it are the research center and hospital. Tulsa is also an arts center, with its own ballet company, opera, and symphony orchestra. It has some fine museums, including an Institute of American History and Art.

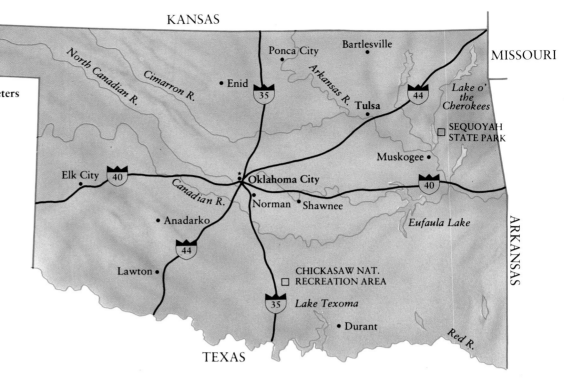

COLORADO

NEW MEXICO

△ Black Mesa
4,973 ft (1,517 m)

KANSAS

MISSOURI

Ponca City • Bartlesville

• Enid

North Canadian R.

Cimarron R.

Arkansas R.

35

Tulsa

44

Lake o' the Cherokees

SEQUOYAH STATE PARK

Muskogee •

Elk City •

40

Canadian R.

Oklahoma City

• Norman

• Shawnee

40

Eufaula Lake

ARKANSAS

• Anadarko

44

Lawton •

CHICKASAW NAT. RECREATION AREA

35

Lake Texoma

• Durant

Red R.

TEXAS

0 — 100 kilometers
0 — 50 miles

OKLAHOMA OIL

An oil refinery in Oklahoma. The discovery and exploitation of oil made Oklahoma rich before petroleum was drilled in neighboring Texas. The first oil well began production on April 15, 1897, near Bartlesville, and there are now 100,000 wells. Oil wells pump daily even inside Oklahoma City's limits, and wells surround the state Capitol Building. One well had to be drilled at an angle so that oil could be extracted from directly under the building. Oklahoma City was once dubbed "Oil Capital of the World." Oil is also drilled around Tulsa.

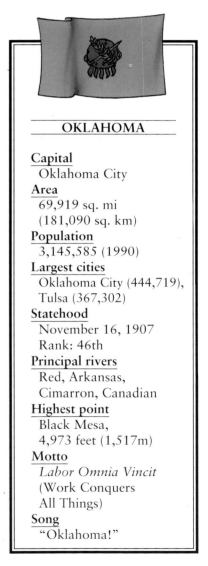

OKLAHOMA

Capital
Oklahoma City
Area
69,919 sq. mi
(181,090 sq. km)
Population
3,145,585 (1990)
Largest cities
Oklahoma City (444,719),
Tulsa (367,302)
Statehood
November 16, 1907
Rank: 46th
Principal rivers
Red, Arkansas,
Cimarron, Canadian
Highest point
Black Mesa,
4,973 feet (1,517m)
Motto
Labor Omnia Vincit
(Work Conquers
All Things)
Song
"Oklahoma!"

CATTLE LANDS

Oklahoma supports some 70,000 farms. Cattle are the state's most valuable agricultural product, and livestock ranks first in terms of farming income. Irrigation schemes have helped farmers keep both their crops and their livestock supplied with water. Although Oklahoma is a serious rival to Texas in oil production, the number of cattle it raises is still less than half the number raised by Texas.

"TRAIL OF TEARS"

The Cherokees were one of the "Five Civilized Tribes" that settled in Oklahoma in the 1830s. This illustration shows the tribes being forced by the U.S. government to move from their original homelands in North Carolina and northern Georgia to what was intended to be a permanent Indian territory, occupying part of present-day Oklahoma. Some 15,000 Cherokees took the "Trail of Tears," on which 4,000 or more died from cold and disease. They were told that the new land was theirs "as long as the grass grows and the waters run." But settlers moved into the territory, outnumbering the Indians by five to one in 1905. Oklahoma was admitted to the Union as a state in 1907.

OREGON

A Pacific Northwest state, Oregon is a land of stunning scenery and vast tracts of timber. It lies north of California, and like California has a long coastline. Unlike Californians, most of whom live along the coast, Oregon's inhabitants live mainly in the fertile inland area of their state, in the Willamette Valley. Also unlike California, most of Oregon's shoreline is public property, open to all. Oregon is the chief timber-producing state of the Union and is mainly rural. Industry is centered around lumber, used for wood and paper products. The redwood tree is perhaps the most valuable hardwood for the construction industry. Most of the state's forests are found in the Cascade and Coast mountain ranges. They are mainly evergreens, including Douglas fir — one of the state's symbols.

Other industries include food processing and the manufacture of scientific instruments. The state also produces a large amount of hydroelectric power. Fruit and vegetables are grown in the Willamette Valley. Wine making is also well established, and the wines of Washington and Yamhill counties in the northwest are rated among the finest in the country. Wheat is the main crop in the eastern half of the state. The Cascade Range, named for its many waterfalls, divides the milder, misty and wet coastal area from the dry, harsher climate of eastern Oregon. In the west, the primary industry is fishing, especially of wild and farmed trout and salmon. Pacific Ocean fishing is as important now as it was to the Chinook tribe that first inhabited the region. Dairy cattle are raised in the Tillamook Valley.

Oregon's spectacular scenery includes the Painted Hills National Monument, the John Day Fossil Beds National Monument, and the spectacular Columbia River Gorge. The mouth of the river was first explored by Lewis and Clark in 1805. Settlers followed in the 1840s, via the famous Oregon Trail, and the land became a U.S. territory in 1849.

CRATER LAKE
Crater Lake is aptly named, as it was formed in a collapsed crater at the summit of an extinct volcano called Mt. Mazama. The lake is a brilliant deep blue color, due to the great depth of the water. It is the centerpiece of the state's only national park. At 1,962 feet (598 m), Crater Lake is the deepest lake in the United States. There is a two-lane highway which goes around a nearby rim offering spectacular views of the lake 2,000 feet (610 m) below.

OREGON	

Capital
Salem
Area
97,073 sq. mi
(251,419 sq. km)
Population
2,842,321 (1990)
Largest cities
Portland (437,319),
Eugene (112,669),
Salem (107,786)
Statehood
February 14, 1859
Rank: 33rd
Principal rivers
Columbia,
Willamette
Highest point
Mt. Hood,
11,239 feet (3,427m)
Motto
She Flies with Her Own
Wings, The Union
Song
"Oregon, My Oregon"

Oregon grape

STATE
SYMBOLS

*Western
meadowlark*

Douglas fir

PORTLAND
The largest city in the state is Portland, which straddles the Willamette River. It is often called the "City of Roses," because it has an abundance of parks with beds of roses — and also rhododendrons. On a clear day, by the riverfront, you can see the state's highest point, Mt. Hood, as well as the volcano Mt. St. Helens which lies in Washington state, and which erupted with terrifying force on May 18, 1980. The explosion was said to be 500 times as powerful as the atomic bomb dropped on Hiroshima. Portland offers several museums and a large zoo.

MT. HOOD

At 11,239 feet (3,427 m) Mt. Hood is the highest mountain in Oregon. Here its snow-covered peak towers in the distance beyond a typical apple orchard in full bloom. Mt. Hood is part of the Cascade Range, which has high slopes covered with evergreen forests. The mountain lies 45 miles (72 km) from Portland and is a dormant volcano which last erupted in 1865. It was first sighted by an English navigator, William Broughton, who named it after the British admiral Lord Hood.

THE OREGON TRAIL

The historic Oregon Trail was an important route for settlers making their way west on horseback or by covered wagon in the 1840s–1870s. It stretches 2,000 miles (3,200 km) from Independence, Missouri, across the Great Plains and Rocky Mountains into the present state of Oregon. Fur trappers and traders established part of the trail around the beginning of the 1800s. They were followed by missionaries and many other settlers, who were lured by the farming opportunities of the Willamette Valley. The end of the trail is marked by a stone in The Dalles, on the northern Oregon border.

GOLDEN EAGLE

The Pacific coast and interior wilderness of Oregon are ideal habitats for the golden eagle. It prefers the open, mountainous country that is typical of this state. This eagle is not really gold in color, but has a few flecks of gold on its neck.

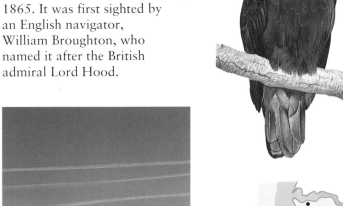

STATE OF FLOWERS

Vivid yellow and red tulips grow in this nursery farm below the snow-capped Mt. Hood in the distance. Flower growing is an important part of the Oregon economy, especially in the Willamette Valley region. Other crops grown by farmers include cranberries, filberts, walnuts, and pears. Visitors drive along the many highways to see Oregon's flowers, parks, and spectacular mountain and coastal scenery.

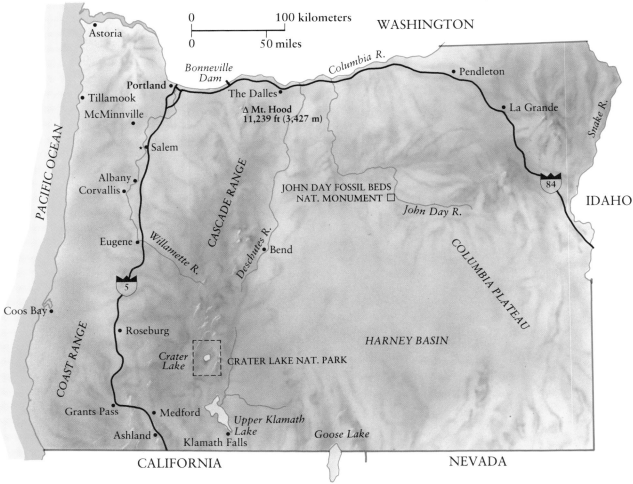

PENNSYLVANIA

The Northeastern state of Pennsylvania is crisscrossed by both the Appalachian and Allegheny mountains, and borders Lake Erie. It is one of the top five industrial states in the Union, particularly in mining, and also has the fifth-highest population in the country. Because of its central location, with six states to the north and six to the south, Pennsylvania has the nickname "Keystone State."

In manufacturing, Pennsylvania remains best known for its steel output. Pittsburgh, in the western part of the state, is the leading steel city in the United States, despite feeling the effects of an economic slump in the late 1970s and early 1980s. The state had its first steel mill, established by the industrialist Andrew Carnegie, in 1853. It also had the first developed oil field, and in the following decades Pennsylvania became a major industrial area, manufacturing iron, steel, arms, and machinery. Pennsylvania's mineral products include Portland cement, stone, pig iron, and lime. It is also one of the country's leading glassmaking states. The state produces automobiles and is the leading producer in the country of frozen dairy products, including ice cream. Other food products made in Pennsylvania include beer and chocolates. In recent years, the state has also developed nuclear power. On March 28, 1979, the first serious nuclear accident in the United States occurred at Three Mile Island, on the Susquehanna River, requiring a total shutdown of the power plant.

Dutch and Swedish settlers were the first Europeans in the region, but in 1682 an English colony was founded by William Penn for the Quakers, a Protestant sect seeking religious freedom. He founded Philadelphia, the largest city in Pennsylvania, and fifth-largest in the nation. Penn's name for the city means "city of brotherly love" in Greek. Philadelphia's Independence Hall was the meeting place of the Continental Congress, which issued the Declaration of Independence — signed on July 4, 1776 — and directed the war effort. Here, too, the U.S. Constitution was drawn up in 1787. From 1790 to 1800 the city served as the nation's first capital.

GETTYSBURG ADDRESS

On November 19, 1863, President Abraham Lincoln delivered his most famous speech, the Gettysburg Address. The speech, which lasted only about two minutes, was given to dedicate a cemetery at Gettysburg for the soldiers who had died in the battle there in July of that year. Lincoln eloquently expressed the reasons for fighting the Civil War, ending with the words "... that government of the people, by the people, for the people, shall not perish from the earth."

STATE SYMBOLS

Hemlock

Mountain laurel

Ruffed grouse

LIBERTY BELL

The Liberty Bell stands in Liberty Bell Pavilion, which was built for Philadelphia's Bicentennial celebrations in 1976. The bell itself was cast in London to commemorate 50 years of Pennsylvania as a colony. It reached Philadelphia in 1752, and one month later was cracked by a stroke of its clapper. It was recast by a local firm and later used to announce that the Continental Congress was in session, and to proclaim the first public reading of the Declaration of Independence. It suffered another crack in 1835. It was not recast because of its historic importance.

PENNSYLVANIA

Capital
Harrisburg
Area
45,308 sq. mi
(117,348 sq. km)
Population
11,881,643 (1990)
Largest cities
Philadelphia (1,585,577),
Pittsburgh (369,879),
Erie (108,718)
Statehood
December 12, 1787
Rank: 2nd
Principal rivers
Allegheny, Ohio,
Susquehanna, Delaware
Highest point
Mt. Davis,
3,213 feet (980 m)
Motto
Virtue, Liberty, and
Independence
Song
None

PITTSBURGH

Skyscrapers, such as this impressive example, dominate the Pittsburgh skyline. One Pittsburgh skyscraper, the U.S. Steel Building, is the tallest between New York City and Chicago. There is a mass of skyscrapers in the Golden Triangle, where the Allegheny, Monongahela, and Ohio rivers meet.

AMISH WAYS

An Amish couple transport their harvest in the traditional, non-mechanized way of their sect. The Amish do not use automobiles, tractors, electricity, or any modern machinery. They live and work simply, gathering to worship at each other's houses twice a week. Amish people are not allowed to hold public office, swear oaths, or join the army. They are descendants of German immigrants from the Rhine region, who settled in large numbers in the inland counties, such as Lancaster. By the time of the Revolutionary War, these Germans were known as Pennsylvania Dutch. The word "Dutch" was taken from *deutsch*, meaning German (not people from The Netherlands). The Amish are just one — albeit the best known — of the German religious sects that settled in Pennsylvania.

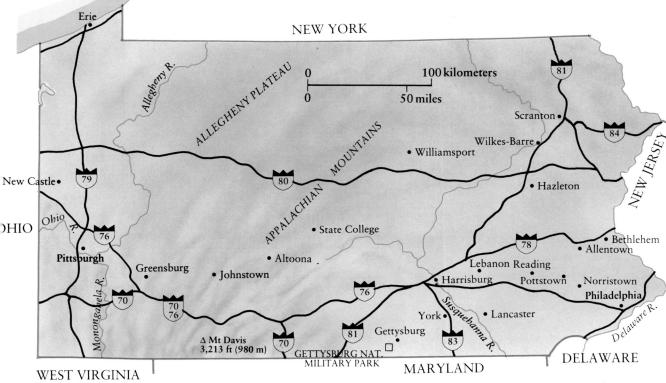

MARY CASSATT

The painter Mary Cassatt was born in Pittsburgh, Pennsylvania in 1844, but moved to France when she was 22 years old. There she studied with the famous Impressionist painters, including Edgar Degas. She worked chiefly in pastels and made many fine figure studies of young women and mothers. This is her tender study of *Mother and Child*. Many of her works were of motherhood. She persuaded some of her wealthy American friends to buy Impressionist paintings and so helped to influence American art appreciation.

PUMPKIN PRODUCER

Pennsylvania is one of the leading pumpkin producers east of the Mississippi River. Freshly harvested pumpkins are shipped out for use either as cattle feed or for human consumption — particularly the pulp, which is boiled or baked in pies, traditionally served at Thanksgiving. Pumpkins are closely related to cucumbers, squashes, and melons.

RHODE ISLAND

The smallest state in the nation, Rhode Island measures a mere 48 miles (77 km) from north to south, and 37 miles (60 km) from east to west. But its population density — the number of people for each square mile — is the second highest in the United States. Some 75 percent of the population live within 15 miles (24 km) of the capital and largest city, Providence. This city is the second largest in New England, after Boston, and is located in the eastern part of the state, at the head of Narragansett Bay. Around one third of the population works in the manufacturing industries, making Rhode Island one of the most industrialized states in the nation. Textiles, metal-working machinery, chemicals, plastics, electrical equipment, silverware, and costume jewelry are the main products. The state leads the world in the manufacture of the latter two items. Textiles once accounted for half the state income, but competition from southern mills and from overseas reduced this. One of Rhode Island's symbols is the Rhode Island Red chicken, bred there from 1857, and a producer of excellent eggs. Small dairy farms and nurseries are other significant agricultural activities, and potatoes, corn, apples, and peaches are also grown.

GRAND MANSIONS
America's richest families built grand French- and Italian-style mansions (their summer houses) along a 3-mile (5-km) cliff stretch of Newport, Rhode Island. The families — the Astors, Vanderbilts, and Belmonts — had made their wealth from the large-scale industrialization of the nation in the 1800s. Typical of these "cottages" (as their owners called them) is The Breakers (above) designed for the industrialist Cornelius Vanderbilt and his family.

The colony of Rhode Island was founded by Roger Williams, who had been expelled from the Massachusetts Bay Colony in 1636. Several denominations built their first houses of worship there. The Touro Synagogue, which was built in 1763 in Newport, is the oldest synagogue in the United States. In 1776, Rhode Island was the first colony to formally declare its independence from England, but the last of the original Thirteen Colonies to join the new Union.

STATE SYMBOLS

Violet

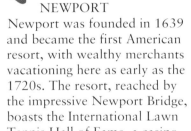

Red maple

Rhode Island Red

NEWPORT
Newport was founded in 1639 and became the first American resort, with wealthy merchants vacationing here as early as the 1720s. The resort, reached by the impressive Newport Bridge, boasts the International Lawn Tennis Hall of Fame, a casino, and the White Horse Tavern, claimed as the country's oldest.

FOUNDERS OF RHODE ISLAND
In 1636, Roger Williams established Rhode Island's first permanent settlement at Providence. Williams was a Puritan minister who was driven out of Massachusetts because he attacked the Puritan leaders for not practicing religious tolerance. Providence was built on land Williams bought from two Narragansett chiefs. Setting up a new colony was fraught with dangers — land had to be cleared even in the harsh New England winter, and supplies were scarce. By 1643, there were four settlements in Rhode Island and Williams suggested that they unite for protection against neighboring colonies. In 1663, King Charles II of England granted Rhode Island a charter under which the settlements united. This charter remained the law of Rhode Island until 1843.

RHODE ISLAND

Capital
Providence
Area
1,212 sq. mi
(3,139 sq. km)
Population
1,003,464 (1990)
Largest cities
Providence (160,728),
Warwick (85,427),
Cranston (76,060)
Statehood
May 29, 1790
Rank: 13th
Principal rivers
Providence, Blackstone
Highest point
Jerimoth Hill,
812 feet (248m)
Motto
Hope
Song
"Rhode Island"

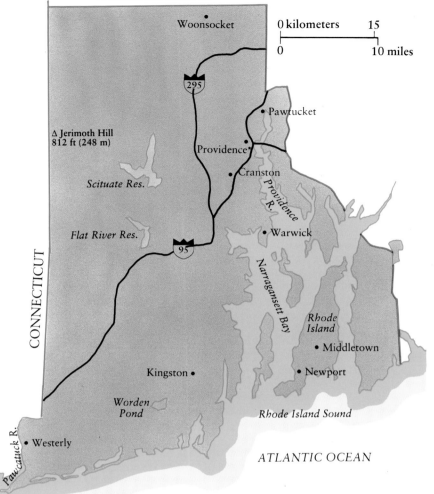

CENTER FOR SAILING
Newport Harbor, Rhode Island, is a yachting center, and many yacht races are held there, including some of the world-famous America's Cup races. In late June there is the annual Block Island Race, and the Newport to Bermuda and Annapolis to Newport races. Sport fishing is also popular in the Ocean State. The waters off Rhode Island provide large fish such as tuna, and smaller fish such as mackerel and bluefish.

COASTAL BIRDS
Gulls and terns are common along Rhode Island's shoreline. The herring gull is the best-known gull in the United States. The Caspian tern is smaller and faster.

Caspian tern

Herring gull

PAWTUCKET
Copper wiring is processed at Pawtucket, close to Providence, the capital of Rhode Island. Pawtucket is a major producer of textiles, machinery, and plastics, as well as copper wire. It is also a center for high-tech industries and toy manufacture.

BROWN UNIVERSITY
The oldest institution of higher education in the state is Brown University. It was founded in 1764, as Rhode Island College, for Baptist men. It began to admit women in 1971. Brown is a private institution and one of the so-called Ivy League colleges. Computer and information sciences, engineering, languages, mathematics, and psychology are among the subjects taught there. The first schools in Rhode Island were set up and supported financially by the main towns. State-supported colleges include the University of Rhode Island at Kingston, and Rhode Island School of Design. The latter is world famous.

SOUTH CAROLINA

One of the original 13 states of the Union, South Carolina is located in the southeastern United States. It is shaped roughly like a triangle, and has a 187-mile (301-km) Atlantic coastline. Georgia lies on its southwest border, while North Carolina runs along its north and northeast border. South Carolina has played a key role in American history: it led the Southern states in breaking away from the Union and into the Civil War. The shots fired at Fort Sumter, in Charleston harbor in 1861, sparked off the war. The state's wealth came from its slave-based rice, indigo and cotton trade, and the wealth of the planters was equal to that of the northern industrialists. Charleston itself was badly damaged in the Civil War, but many of the wealthy merchants' mansions have been restored. The gardens of the old Charleston homes are at their best in spring, when the magnolias and other flowers come into bloom. Charleston Museum, established in 1773, is the oldest in the United States. There is also an Old Slave Museum which is the oldest museum devoted to black culture. It vividly evokes the horrors of slave trading, depicting shackled slaves coming off their crammed ships. Nearby is Charles Towne Landing — named after the English King Charles II — where the first British colonists settled in 1670. These settlers were mainly poor whites from Barbados, who managed only a precarious existence. Later, exiled Huguenots (French Protestants) arrived and started rice plantations, worked by slave labor. The invention of the cotton gin in 1793 established cotton as the leading crop until the Civil War.

The coastal plain covers two-thirds of the state. In the northwest corner are the Blue Ridge Mountains. The rest of the state is part of the Piedmont Plateau. South Carolina has a hot, humid climate favoring the cultivation of tobacco and soybeans, as well as corn, cotton, and peaches.

SOUTH CAROLINA

Capital
Columbia
Area
31,113 sq. mi
(80,583 sq. km)
Population
3,486703 (1990)
Largest cities
Columbia (98,052),
Charleston (80,414)
Statehood
May 23, 1788
Rank: 8th
Principal river
Santee, Edisto,
Savannah
Highest point
Sassafras Mountain,
3,560 feet (1,086m)
Motto
Dum Spiro Spero
(While I Breathe, I Hope)
Song
"Carolina"

CHARLESTON
Many restored old houses along Charleston's harbor were built in the 1700s for sea captains and merchants. Charleston is a busy port and the largest city in the eastern lowland area. It was the first permanent settlement in what is now South Carolina. It started as Charles Towne, in 1670, and was moved to its present location between the Ashley and Cooper rivers ten years later.

STATE SYMBOLS

Carolina wren

Palmetto

Carolina jessamine

TABLE ROCK
A mountain lake in northwest South Carolina reflects Table Rock, part of the Blue Ridge chain of the Appalachian Mountains. The Blue Ridge region is a small area tucked away in the far northwest corner. It offers spectacular scenery but does not contribute to the state's economy. The Blue Ridge Mountains enter from North Carolina and contain Sassafras Mountain, at 3,560 feet (1,086 m) the state's highest peak.

THE TEXTILE STATE
A typical garment factory in South Carolina. Textiles and clothing are important manufactured goods in this cotton-growing state. However, the textile industry depends less on cotton today than on synthetic fibers such as nylon and rayon. The state has supported schools to train workers for this industry — there were over 400 such establishments in the 1980s, employing about 30 percent of the textile work force. Textile mills are concentrated in the northwest of the state. The industry began in the 1820s when cotton was firmly established as the state's foremost crop, grown on large plantations.

KIAWAH ISLAND
This large island, part of a coastal chain of barrier islands, is not far from Charleston, and includes wildlife refuge areas, forests, marshlands, and isolated beaches, as well as a historic private mansion. In 1991 the island was also the site of the Ryder Cup, a golf tournament held every two years in which a team of the best of America's golfers takes on the best golfing team from all parts of Europe. Apart from trying to win the trophy for their team, the golfers also had to keep an eye out for the many alligators that lurk around the golf course greens and fairways.

PEACHES
One of the state's main crops is peaches. They were introduced by Spanish explorers. Cultivated fruit trees thrive in the state's warm climate.

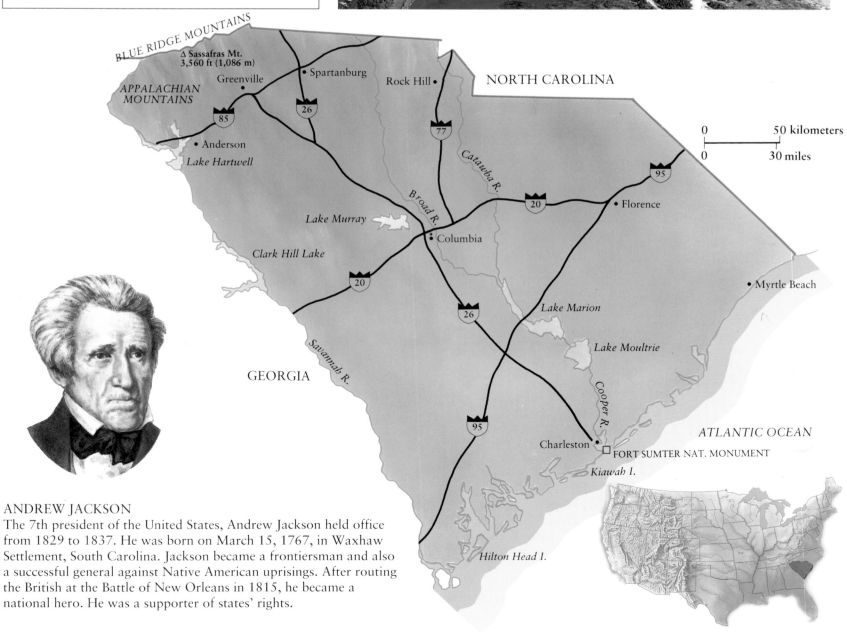

ANDREW JACKSON
The 7th president of the United States, Andrew Jackson held office from 1829 to 1837. He was born on March 15, 1767, in Waxhaw Settlement, South Carolina. Jackson became a frontiersman and also a successful general against Native American uprisings. After routing the British at the Battle of New Orleans in 1815, he became a national hero. He was a supporter of states' rights.

SOUTH DAKOTA

Geographically South Dakota is almost like two states divided down the center by the Missouri River. East of the Missouri is rich, rolling farmland where farmers grow corn, wheat, soybeans, and alfalfa. But there are also glacial lakes to the north. West of the Missouri is seemingly endless prairie with few trees. It is here, to the southwest, that South Dakota's most elevated region, the Black Hills, lies. These hills extend for some 120 miles (193 km) from north to south and 60 miles (97 km) from east to west; their granite peaks rise 4,000 feet (1,200 m) above the surrounding plains. Mt. Rushmore is located here. Next to the Black Hills are the barren but stunning Badlands, a region of jagged cliffs and ravines. The largest area of Badlands in South Dakota lies between the Cheyenne and White rivers. As in neighboring North Dakota, the weather is harsh, with hot summers and cold winters. There is a feeling of open space throughout this sparsely populated state, and over 90 percent of the land is suitable for farming. However, the state suffers from periodic drought, frosts, and blizzards. It also felt the full force of the "Dust Bowl" of the 1930s when severe winds whipped off the fertile topsoil and brought great suffering to the people of the state. Today, South Dakota's agriculture is thriving. Livestock raising, especially of beef cattle, is important to western South Dakota. The territory of South Dakota was obtained from the French in 1803, as part of the Louisiana Purchase. It was traditionally Sioux territory, and until the 1870s, when gold was discovered, it attracted relatively few settlers — mainly fur traders and farmers.

CUSTER STATE PARK
A bison mother suckles her calf unperturbed in Custer State Park, an area of mountains, forests, and lakes. Other animals found in the park include antelope, deer, and elk, all of which roam the range.

CALAMITY JANE
Martha Jane Burke was a frontierswoman who, under the nickname of Calamity Jane, became a famous Wild West character. In 1876 she moved to Deadwood, South Dakota, and became a bullwhacker, hauling goods to the gold mining camps.

GIANT SCULPTURES
The heads of four presidents are carved in the side of Mt. Rushmore in the Black Hills of South Dakota. This "Shrine of Democracy," as it is known, is part of Mt. Rushmore National Memorial. The faces are 70 feet (21 m) high. Visitors approach the sculpted heads along a scenic route called the Iron Mountain Road, which zigzags up steep slopes with several bridges and tunnels.

Ringed-necked pheasant

STATE SYMBOLS

American pasqueflower

Black Hills spruce

SOUTH DAKOTA

Capital
Pierre
Area
77,116 sq. mi
(199,730 sq. km)
Population
696,004 (1990)
Largest cities
Sioux Falls (100,814),
Rapid City (54,523,
Aberdeen (24,927)
Statehood
November 2, 1889
Rank: 40th
Principal rivers
Cheyenne, White,
Missouri
Highest point
Harney Peak,
7,242 feet (2,209 m)
Motto
Under God, the People
Rule
Song
"Hail, South Dakota"

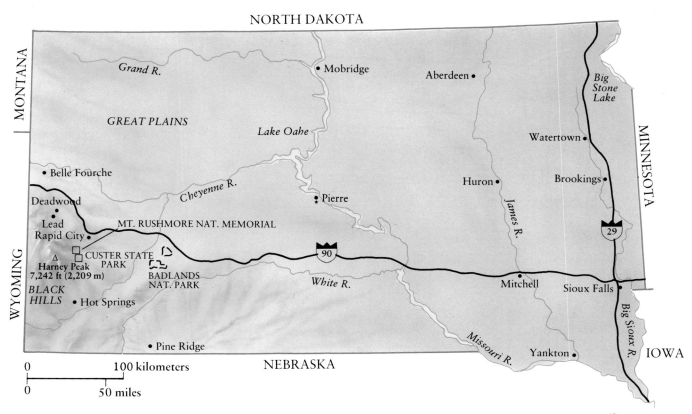

DAKOTA
Dakota, or "allies", was the name the Sioux gave themselves and tribes friendly to them. Today the Sioux make up over 7 percent of South Dakota's population. This man is dressed in the traditional costume of the Sioux.

MAMMOTH REMAINS
Visitors inspect the remains of extinct Ice Age mammoths at Mammoth Site, Hot Springs, in the southwest corner of South Dakota. Mammoth bones that have been preserved for 10,000 years are on display at this site. The mammoth was a prehistoric relative of the elephant. It existed until relatively recently, dying out a mere 10,000 years ago. Earlier animals that roamed the North American continent include brontotheres, which looked similar to a rhinoceros, saber-toothed cats, and ancestors of pronghorn antelopes, pigs, sheep, and cattle. Hot Springs itself is suitably named for its large, still-bubbling springs. The Sioux fought the Cheyenne over the land rights for these springs.

PRAIRIE DOGS
As its name suggests, the prairie dog is found on the prairies, particularly on the plains of South Dakota. It is a type of squirrel that lives in the ground in large groups known as colonies, or "towns." In their underground colonies, linked by a network of tunnels, the animals groom each other and appear to kiss. If an enemy such as a rattlesnake or coyote comes close, the prairie dogs will warn others in the colony with loud, sharp, barking calls. The openings to the burrows are surrounded by mounds of earth to prevent the burrows from flooding.

GOLD MINING
A miner at work in a South Dakota gold mine. The Homestake Mine, just north of Rapid City, in western South Dakota, is the most profitable gold mine in the United States. Surface tours are available for sightseers. Mining in general, however, makes up only a very small percentage of the state's income. There are many old "gold rush" towns where the mines are no longer working. Some of these are open to visitors.

TENNESSEE

A land of music and mountains, Tennessee is a long, narrow Southern state lying in the east-central part of the United States. It extends from the Great Smoky Mountains in eastern Tennessee over 432 miles (695 km) to the Mississippi River. Tennessee is bordered by eight states: to the north are Kentucky and Virginia; to the south Georgia, Alabama, and Mississippi; to the west lie Missouri and Arkansas; and to the east is North Carolina. The Great Smoky Mountains have magnificent plants and wildlife, and are crisscrossed with white-water creeks and rivers. The construction of a number of dams on the Tennessee River was a project of the Tennessee Valley Authority (TVA), an agency set up and financed by the federal government as part of the New Deal during the Depression of the 1930s. The project tamed the Tennessee River and provided plentiful power for industry, and the dams formed a number of lakes, including Cherokee Lake.

TENNESSEE
Capital
Nashville
Area
42,144 sq. mi
(109,152 sq. km)
Population
4,887,185 (1990)
Largest cities
Memphis (610,337),
Nashville–Davidson
(488,374),
Knoxville (165,121)
Statehood
June 1, 1796
Rank: 16th
Principal rivers
Tennessee, Mississippi
Highest point
Clingmans Dome,
6,643 feet (2,026m)
Motto
Agriculture and
Commerce
Song
"The Tennessee Waltz"

Once a mainly rural state known chiefly for its dairy products, Tennessee has become increasingly industrialized. Chemicals and machinery are the primary products, and there is also a large cottonseed-oil business based in Memphis, the largest city. In the past, Tennessee's main crop was cotton; but it has been surpassed by soybeans and tobacco. There is cattle raising in the state, as well as breeding of the Tennessee Walking horse, a famous breed of saddle horse. There is also an automobile industry, and an important center for nuclear research at Oak Ridge. Tourism is a thriving industry in the state. Vacationers come to see the beautiful countryside, and enjoy the states musical heritage. Tennessee is both the birth place of the blues and the capital of country and western music. During the Civil War the state was the site of many battles.

STATE SYMBOLS

Mockingbird

Iris

Tulip poplar

NASHVILLE SKYLINE
Tennessee's capital occupies hilly ground along the Cumberland River near the center of the state. It is best known as the home of American country and western music. The Grand Ole Opry House, a large concert hall, has presented many of the most famous country and western artists including Roy Rogers, Johnny Cash, and Dolly Parton.

ELVIS PRESLEY
Elvis Aaron Presley was born in Tupelo, Mississippi, but after achieving fame, he settled on a vast estate called Graceland, in Memphis. He died in the mansion on August 16, 1977. Eight million of his records were sold in the week after his death. Elvis was the supreme performer of the Rock'n'Roll music of the mid-1950s. The studios of Sun Records, where Elvis and other artists launched the songs that were to transform the sound and look of popular music, are in Memphis.

AUTOMOBILES
Several new, large, high-tech motor vehicle plants have been built near Nashville, including some making Japanese automobiles, such as these Nissan trucks. Trucks and cars from Japan have cut greatly into the sales and production of American cars. Other Nashville industries include food processing, glassmaking, and recordings. More than 180 record companies are located here.

WILD TURKEYS
The wild turkey is a native bird of North America. It lives in woodlands in parts of the central, southern, and eastern United States, including Tennessee as well as North Carolina and Minnesota. It is a different species from the domestic turkey, traditionally served for Thanksgiving and Christmas dinners.

ATHENS OF THE SOUTH
Nashville is sometimes referred to as the "Athens of the South" because of its many colleges and universities and for its Greek Revival architecture — buildings that copy the style of the Ancient Greek cities. Located in Centennial Park, this building is the world's only full-scale replica of the Parthenon temple in Athens, Greece.

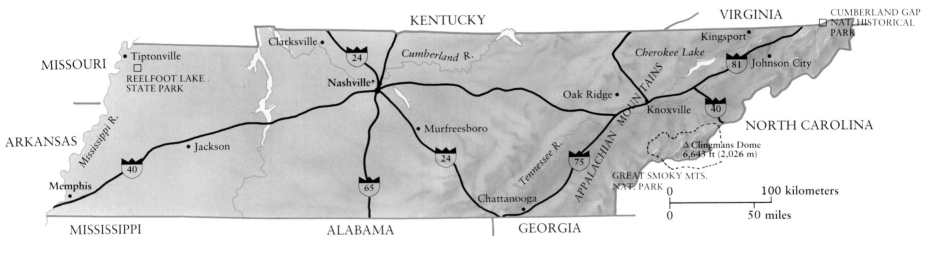

CUMBERLAND GAP
Pinnacle Overlook, in the Cumberland Gap National Historical Park, offers spectacular views. At this point the borders of three states — Kentucky, Virginia, and Tennessee — meet. Cold, moist air, or mist, trapped by the Great Smoky Mountains, often sweeps over the peaks. The mountains are part of the great Appalachian chain which extends from Canada in the north to Alabama in the south. Many pioneers passed through the Gap when moving west in the early 1700s and 1800s.

TEXAS

Texas was the largest state in the Union until 1959, when Alaska became a state. It was also credited with the largest underground oil lake in the United States until larger reserves were discovered in Alaska. Texas remains the largest of the 48 contiguous states, and oil has made Texas among the richest states in the nation. It was at Spindletop, Texas, that the state's first great oil "gusher" erupted from the ground on January 10, 1901. It uncovered one of the most productive oil fields in the world. Today Texas leads all other states in the production of its most important natural resources — petroleum and cotton. The state also leads the world in oil-disaster rescue and cleanup operations, from tanker spillages to the burning oil wells of Kuwait sabotaged by Iraqi forces in the Persian Gulf War of 1991. Dallas is another oil city and is the banking center of the Southwest. The Dallas–Fort Worth area is a center for manufacturing, aerospace, and the electronics industry. Texas, however, is more than just oil wells and Stetson-hatted oilmen; it is also one of the most productive farming states in the Union. Cattle and cotton dominated the state before oil was discovered. In the past, much of the farm work was done by black slaves and Mexicans – whose descendants, along with newcomers, form a sizeable portion of today's population. Texas is a leading center for the nation's space flight programs. NASA's Lyndon B. Johnson Space Center in Houston was the "mission control" for the Mercury, Gemini, and Apollo space flights.

As a republic, Texas acquired the flag it still flies today — a red, white, and blue flag bearing a single star — the inspiration for its nickname, "Lone Star State."

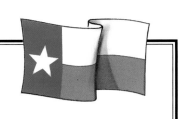

TEXAS

Capital
Austin
Area
266,807 sq. mi
(691,030 sq. km)
Population
16,986,510 (1990)
Largest cities
Houston (1,630,553),
Dallas (1,006,877),
San Antonio (935,933),
El Paso (515,342)
Statehood
December 29, 1845
Rank: 28th
Principal rivers
Rio Grande, Red, Brazos
Highest point
Guadalupe Peak,
8,749 feet (2,668 m)
Motto
Friendship
Song
"Texas, Our Texas"

TEXAS BECOMES A STATE

The American flag was raised on Texas soil in 1845. Before this time, Texas had been a possession of Spain, then of Mexico, and then an independent republic. President James K. Polk was instrumental in acquiring Texas for the United States. The annexation of Texas and a dispute over the Texas–Mexico border triggered the Mexican War of 1846–48.

THE ALAMO

The Alamo was built by the Spanish as a mission in 1718. In 1835-6 the people of Texas rebelled against the Mexican government who ruled over Texas. The Mexican army led by General Santa Anna, marched on San Antonio. The Texans retreated to the Alamo and a long siege followed. The Mexicans finally took the fort on March 6, 1836. Many died, including frontiersmen Davy Crockett, Jim Bowie, and William Travis.

STATE SYMBOLS

Mockingbird

Pecan

Bluebonnet

DALLAS

Dallas is the second-largest city in Texas with over a million people. Glass-clad skyscrapers testify to the enormous wealth of the city, derived from oil, cattle, insurance, and other industries. Dallas is also home to the Texas State Fair, the largest of its kind in the nation.

ARMADILLO

The only armadillo in the United States is the Texas armadillo. It is also known as the nine-banded armadillo because it is covered with nine thin, bony plates joined together to form a kind of armor. It feeds at night on insects and worms.

OIL PUMPS

After the eruption of a huge oil gusher in 1901, three more oil fields were found in Texas in the early 1900s. In 1930 the great East Texas oil field was discovered — at that time the largest oil lake in the nation. Oil and natural gas provide the raw materials for a very large petrochemical industry.

PRESIDENT JOHNSON

Lyndon B. Johnson was born in Stonewall, Texas, in what is now Lyndon B. Johnson National Historic Park. His boyhood home is there, and open to sightseers. He was the 30th president, taking office after the assassination of John F. Kennedy in Dallas, Texas, in 1963. Johnson pushed the country fully into the Vietnam War, with no positive results, but also initiated the "Great Society" reforms to aid the nation's underprivileged.

HOUSTON

Houston is the fourth-largest city in the United States, and a leading seaport and space center. The Houston metropolitan area is the nation's leader in the manufacture of petrochemicals and oil field equipment. It bustles with oil, steel, and cotton businesses. The city was founded in 1836 and named after General Sam Houston, hero of the Texan War of Independence. The Houston Ship Canal connects the city with the Gulf of Mexico 50 miles (80 km) away.

UTAH

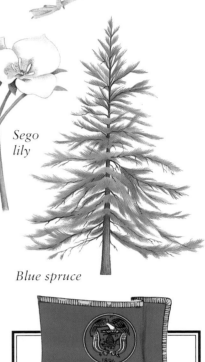

Seagull

Sego lily

Blue spruce

L ying in the heart of the Rocky Mountains, Utah has a generally high elevation, with many high peaks; even its lowest point is 2,000 feet (610 m) above sea level. At its southeast corner, it meets three other states — New Mexico, Colorado, and Arizona. Utah is famous for its spectacular national parks, of which the best known are Bryce Canyon, Zion, and Arches. The strange rugged rock formations of these parks resulted from the action of the large glaciers that formed in prehistoric times, and from erosion caused by flash floods pouring over the bare rocks. The Great Salt Lake, in the northwest of the state, is all that remains of what was once a vast inland sea.

Most of Utah is mountainous or semidesert. The arid Great Basin, which includes Great Salt Lake, occupies the western third. The rest of the state consists of the Rockies in the north, and the Colorado Plateau in the south. The state produces a number of valuable minerals including oil, natural gas, coal, copper, iron ore, gold, and silver. Steel making, copper smelting, and oil refining are the main manufacturing activities. Utah's many farms and ranches have cattle and sheep, which are raised as livestock. Market dairy products are also important.

Fur trappers were among the first travelers in the region. The Mormons arrived in 1848, the year in which Utah became part of the United States as a result of the Mexican War. The region became a territory in 1850, with the Mormon leader Brigham Young as governor. It was named Utah after the Ute Indians who lived there along with Shoshone and Paiute tribes. The Mormons had called the region *Deseret*, a Mormon word meaning honeybee, which stands for hard work and industry. This is where Utah gets its nickname, the "Beehive State." In 1890 the church gave up the practice of polygamy, which allowed a man to have more than one wife, and this opened the way for Utah to become a state in 1896. Today the population is chiefly of European descent, the result of several Mormon migrations. Most people in the state live in a narrow belt stretching from Ogden to Provo.

MORMON CITY
The six-spired Mormon Temple in Salt Lake City, capital of Utah and world center of the Mormon Church, took 40 years to build. Utah's story is linked to that of the Church of Jesus Christ of Latter-Day Saints.

BRYCE CANYON
Bryce Canyon National Park, in the southern part of Utah, was the state's first national park. Its pink cliffs, colored by iron and other minerals in the limestone, are spectacular and reveal layers of sediment deposits laid down over millions of years. The Paiute word for Bryce means "red rocks standing like men in a bowl-shaped canyon."

UTAH	
Capital	
Salt Lake City	
Area	
84,899 sq. mi	
(219,888 sq. km).	
Population	
1,722,850 (1990)	
Largest cities	
Salt Lake City (159,936),	
West Valley City	
(86,976)	
Statehood	
January 4, 1896	
Rank: 45th	
Principal rivers	
Colorado, Green	
Highest point	
Kings Peak,	
13,528 feet (4,126 m)	
Motto	
Industry	
Song	
"Utah, We Love Thee"	

COPPER MINE
Bingham Canyon is the site of the Kennecott open-pit copper mine — the largest in the world. This area of north-central Utah is rich in minerals, including coal, gold, silver, lead, uranium, and molybdenum. Copper is one of the most important minerals mined in Utah, and is used in building and construction, electric and electronic manufacturing, and by industrial machinery and equipment makers. The U.S. is the world's second-largest producer.

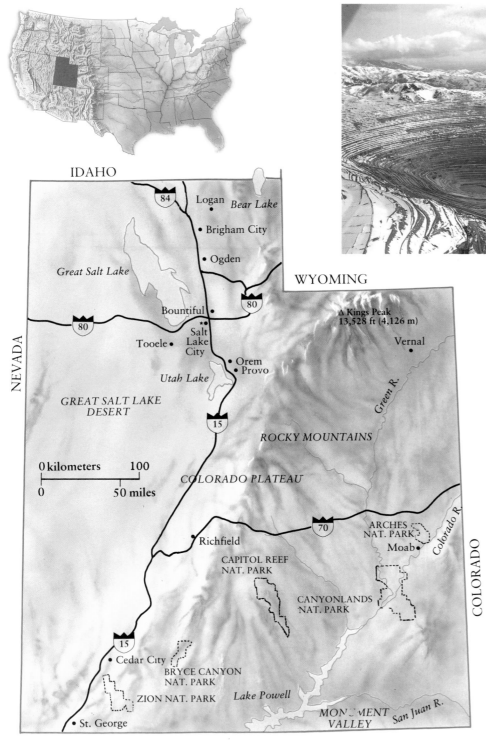

BOBCATS
Bobcats thrive in the mountain forests and stony terrain of the Rocky Mountain states, and Utah provides these habitats in abundance. Also called the lynx, the bobcat generally hunts at night, feeding on rodents, rabbits, birds, and sometimes deer.

THE MORMON TRAIL
In July 1847, Brigham Young, the Mormons' leader, announced to his followers: "This is the right place" — having led them 1,300 miles (2,000 km) from Illinois. He was standing at what was to become Salt Lake City. To make this dry, salty land fertile, the Mormons created a network of irrigation channels to grow crops.

NEWSPAPER ROCK
Early cave dwellers, called the Anasazi have left amazing rock scratchings, called petroglyphs, at what is now the Newspaper Rock State Historical Monument. The carvings may have been a kind of news report for the inhabitants. Many of the petroglyphs are clearly etched and obvious to the untrained eye — including hands, feet, deer-hunting, mountain sheep, and sun signs. The Navajo word for this rock is *Tsi Haue*, "rock that tells a story." The site is located within Canyonlands National Park. To get there, drivers pass through a narrow, verdant valley with towering sandstone walls.

VERMONT

The name of this New England state, in the northeast corner of the country, comes from the French words *vert* and *mont*, which mean "green mountain" — the state's nickname. The Green Mountains of Vermont run north to south like a backbone along the center of the state. The width of the range varies from 20 to 36 miles (32 to 58 km). The state's many mountain regions yield granite, marble, and other kinds of stone. However, such a rock-filled landscape also prevents farming from playing a major role in the state's economy. The state was first investigated by the French explorer Samuel de Champlain, whose name has been given to a lake and to the canal that links Vermont to the sea by connecting Lake Champlain to the Hudson River in New York state.

Vermont has a small, scattered population, and its countryside is well protected by environmental protection laws, passed as early as the 1970s, which also control all development within the state. There are 40 state parks and 34 state forests. Each year, in the fall, visitors from out of state come to see the leaves turn spectacular shades of red and gold. Long winters and deep snow in the mountains attract many thousands of skiers to the 56 ski areas in the state. The two chief agricultural products are apples and maple syrup. The few thousand farms in the state are located mainly around Lake Champlain in the northwest, or along the Connecticut River, which forms Vermont's eastern boundary. Milk from dairy cows is also a major product. Forests cover much of Vermont and provide the raw material for the state's thriving lumber industry. Quarrying began in the state in 1785, and large deposits of granite, marble, and slate are used in buildings throughout the nation.

Sugar maple

Red clover

COVERED BRIDGE
This typical New England scene, a covered bridge surrounded by thickly wooded hills, is just north of Brattleboro. There are over 100 of these historic bridges in Vermont alone. The largest concentrations of them, totaling 16, can be found around Lamomile County, east of Burlington. Such bridges attract vacationers year-round and help make tourism a major source of Vermont's income. Visitors come to enjoy the state's invigorating climate and clean air, with hundreds of thousands of acres of protected forests, public recreation parks, and wildlife preserves.

STATE SYMBOLS

Hermit thrush

ETHAN ALLEN
In the 1750s, Ethan Allen settled on land that is now in Vermont. This land was later given to New York by the British government. Allen formed the Green Mountain Boys to defend Vermont's land. During the Revolutionary War the Green Mountain Boys captured Fort Ticonderoga from the British.

FALL FOLIAGE AND CHURCH STEEPLES
Such pastoral scenes as this, at Brattleboro in fall, attract thousands of tourists. Brattleboro was formerly Fort Dummer, the first permanent settlement in Vermont. The fort was established to protect early settlers from Indian raids. The brilliant colors of a New England fall are best seen from mid-September to mid-October. Brattleboro, on the Connecticut River, is famous for its organ pipes, which it has been producing since 1853.

GREEN MOUNTAIN STATE

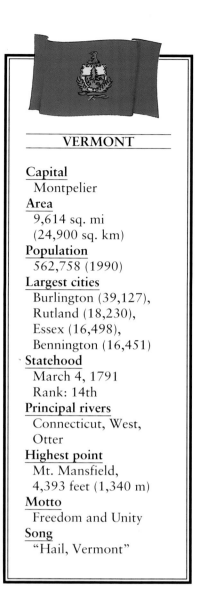

VERMONT

Capital
Montpelier
Area
9,614 sq. mi
(24,900 sq. km)
Population
562,758 (1990)
Largest cities
Burlington (39,127),
Rutland (18,230),
Essex (16,498),
Bennington (16,451)
Statehood
March 4, 1791
Rank: 14th
Principal rivers
Connecticut, West,
Otter
Highest point
Mt. Mansfield,
4,393 feet (1,340 m)
Motto
Freedom and Unity
Song
"Hail, Vermont"

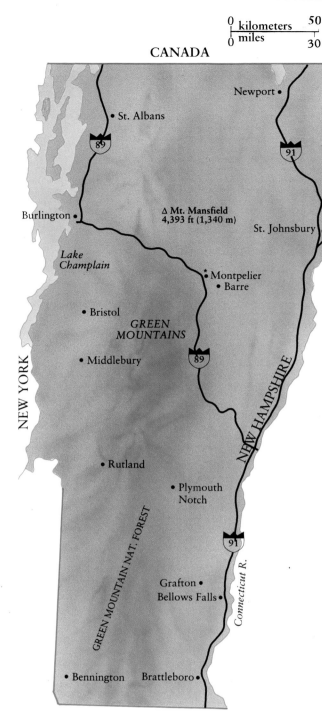

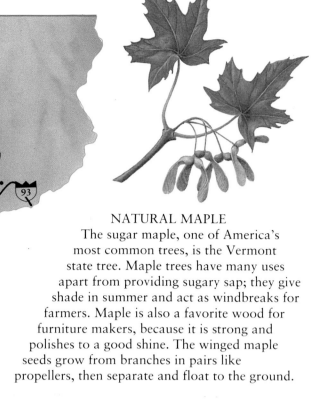

NATURAL MAPLE
The sugar maple, one of America's most common trees, is the Vermont state tree. Maple trees have many uses apart from providing sugary sap; they give shade in summer and act as windbreaks for farmers. Maple is also a favorite wood for furniture makers, because it is strong and polishes to a good shine. The winged maple seeds grow from branches in pairs like propellers, then separate and float to the ground.

EXTRACTING MAPLE SYRUP
As winter turns to spring, the sap in the sugar maples begins to rise, heralding "sugaring time." Millions of trees are tapped for the annual maple syrup harvest. The sap is sugared down in special buildings where the water in the sap boils off in an evaporator. It takes the extract of four trees to produce 1 gallon (3.8 liters) of maple syrup. Because of this, maple syrup is expensive. Several farms — most of which are primarily dairy farms, admit visitors to see the operation of their sugar houses.

CALVIN COOLIDGE
John Calvin Coolidge, 30th president of the United States, was born in Plymouth Notch, Vermont, on July 4, 1872. During his presidency, between 1923 and 1929, the country was generally prosperous, but this ended with the stock market crash of 1929. Coolidge was a man of few words and was called "Silent Cal." Much of his term was dominated by gangsters who fought to control the illegal liquor trade that sprang up during Prohibition.

FALL FESTIVAL
Vermont's Fall Festival celebrates the autumnal transformation of leaf colors. This concert, in an attractive bandstand at Grafton, is typical of the festivities that take place at this time of year. Country fairs and harvest festivals abound in the state, and there are many summer evening open-air band concerts in Vermont towns.

109

VIRGINIA

The East Coast state of Virginia was the first permanent British colonial settlement. It was named after Queen Elizabeth I of England, the "Virgin Queen." But it was King James I who approved the setting up of the first colony at Jamestown on May 14, 1607. Since then, the state has played a key role in the nation's development and history. Virginia extends from Chesapeake Bay in the east to the Allegheny Mountains in the west. The land regions are varied and include the Blue Ridge Mountains, the Piedmont Plateau, and the fertile Tidewater areas, where the Potomac, Rappahannock, York, and James rivers flow into Chesapeake Bay. The most fertile soil is in the Shenandoah Valley. Skyline Drive, through Shenandoah National Park, offers spectacular panoramic views of the surrounding countryside. Virginia is chiefly an agricultural state, whose main crops are tobacco, peanuts, and corn. Richmond, the capital, is a major producer of cigarettes. Tobacco was first cultivated by white settlers in 1612 from seeds brought from the West Indies by one of the colonists. Because it is situated close to Washington, D.C., the nation's capital, Virginia has many federal government buildings and offices providing employment for almost 20 percent of the state's large population.

Virginia has perhaps the greatest number of historical attractions in the United States. To the southeast of Richmond lie Jamestown, site of the first settlement; the restored colonial town of Williamsburg, Virginia's capital between 1699 and 1779; and Yorktown, where the British finally surrendered to the Americans in 1781. Richmond itself was raided by British troops, led by the treacherous Benedict Arnold, earlier that year, and some of its buildings were burned. Richmond also served as the capital of the Confederacy during most of the Civil War.

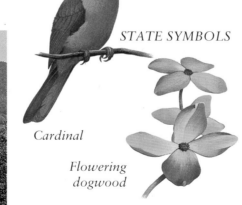

Dogwood

STATE SYMBOLS

Cardinal

Flowering dogwood

ARLINGTON NATIONAL CEMETERY

The Tomb of the Unknowns, where the nation honors its dead from four wars of this century, is at Arlington National Cemetery, Virginia. The tomb itself contains an unidentified World War I soldier. Servicemen from World War II, the Korean War, and the Vietnam War are buried nearby. The cemetery is also the site of this 78-foot high (24-m) bronze statue of U.S. Marines raising the American flag on Iwo Jima Island in the Pacific during World War II. A torch burns night and day over the grave of President John F. Kennedy, who was buried at Arlington in 1963.

TOBACCO FIELDS

Shaded valleys such as this one at Jonesville, Virginia, provide excellent shelter for the state's many tobacco fields. Tobacco, grown in the southern Piedmont, is the chief crop. It was also the earliest colonial crop, first planted by the colony's second leader, John Rolfe, in 1612 near Jamestown. He raised a small crop from seeds he had brought with him from the West Indies. During the 1700s tobacco plantations flourished as slaves were brought in to work on them.

MOUNT VERNON

George Washington's home, Mount Vernon, near Alexandria, is one of Viginia's major historical landmarks. Some of the trees next to the house were planted by Washington himself. The house has wide, sweeping lawns and well-tended grounds with views over the Potomac River. It was Washington's home from 1754–99.

MARYLAND
WASHINGTON D.C.
Potomac R.
Arlington
66
Manassas
Alexandria
SHENANDOAH
NAT. PARK
Fredericksburg
Charlottesville
95
Monticello
64
Rappahannock R.
Richmond
Chesapeake Bay
ATLANTIC
OCEAN
WEST VIRGINIA
James R.
81
KENTUCKY
Petersburg
Williamsburg
Yorktown
Hampton
Newport News
Lynchburg
Roanoke
Appomattox
Norfolk
Virginia Beach
Chesapeake
85
Wytheville
77
Jonesville
Mt. Rogers
5,729 ft (1,746 m)
TENNESSEE
Danville
NORTH CAROLINA

0 — 100 kilometers
0 — 50 miles

ROCK OF AGES
Natural Bridge, near the border with West Virginia, is a 215-foot-high (65-m) limestone arch. It was once owned by Thomas Jefferson, and George Washington climbed it as a young man to mark his initials on the rock.

FIRST PRESIDENT
George Washington, the first U.S. president, was born on February 22, 1732, in Westmoreland County, Virginia. He led the country to victory over British troops in the Revolutionary War. The nation's capital was built near his home, in his honor.

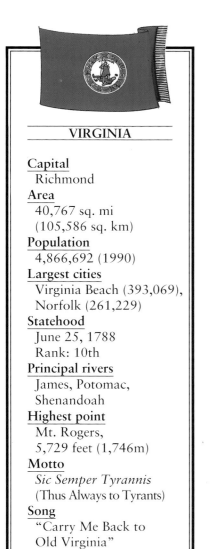

VIRGINIA

Capital
Richmond
Area
40,767 sq. mi
(105,586 sq. km)
Population
4,866,692 (1990)
Largest cities
Virginia Beach (393,069),
Norfolk (261,229)
Statehood
June 25, 1788
Rank: 10th
Principal rivers
James, Potomac,
Shenandoah
Highest point
Mt. Rogers,
5,729 feet (1,746m)
Motto
Sic Semper Tyrannis
(Thus Always to Tyrants)
Song
"Carry Me Back to
Old Virginia"

ROBERT E. LEE
Born into an old Virginia family, Robert E. Lee was the leading general of the Confederacy. Lincoln offered him the job of commanding the Union Army at the start of the Civil War in 1861, but Lee turned it down because he could not, he said, raise his hand against his relatives and his home. When Virginia left the Union, Lee joined the Confederacy. He won several important victories against larger, better-equipped Union armies, but eventually was forced to surrender.

BLUE RIDGE MOUNTAINS
There is plenty of agricultural land in the rolling Piedmont foothills below the peaks of the Blue Ridge Mountains in Virginia. Vast hardwood and conifer forests abound, with cascading streams and rugged cliffs. Wildlife includes bears, deer, bobcats, groundhogs, chipmunks, and 200 species of birds. There are so many types of flowers that they have not yet all been listed. This area attracts many hikers and campers, and extends into North Carolina.

111

WASHINGTON

Suitably named the "Evergreen State," Washington has large regions covered with beautiful Douglas fir, cedar, and spruce woods. The eastern half of the state, however, is a vast area of dry, flat sagebrush desert reclaimed by irrigation. It is now cattle-grazing and wheat-growing country with a continental climate similar to that of the north-Midwestern states. The Cascade Range effectively splits the state from north to south, with the western portion being lush and green, and very wet and cool. About 75 percent of the state's population live in the western region, mostly along the shores of Puget Sound. This is an inlet of the Pacific flanked by the Coast and Cascade mountain ranges. Washington's largest city, Seattle, once the main port for Alaska, lies at the mouth of Puget Sound, and the capital, Olympia, lies at the southern tip of Puget Sound on the Olympic Peninsula. Seen on a map, it may not look like a peninsula, but the Olympia area is surrounded by water on three sides. The Olympic Mountain range dominates the peninsula. Captain George Vancouver, a British sea captain, sailed into the Sound in 1792, and claimed the area for Great Britain. Britain and the United States ruled Washington jointly until 1846. Today, this Pacific Coast state is bordered on the north by the Canadian province of British Columbia, on the east by Idaho, on the south by Oregon, and on the west by the Pacific Ocean. The Columbia River, which rises in Canada and flows southward, is Washington's most important waterway. It is joined by the Snake River as it cuts through eastern Washington and forms the border with Oregon as it bends westward. About halfway down its course lies the Grand Coulee Dam, completed in 1942. It is the largest concrete dam in the United States and is also one of the biggest U.S. hydroelectric projects, providing water for the drier eastern part of the state. Washington is second only to Oregon in lumber production. Its forests yield plywood, paper, cardboard, containers, and furniture.

WASHINGTON	
Capital	Olympia
Area	68,139 sq. mi (176,480 sq. km)
Population	4,866,692 (1990)
Largest cities	Seattle (516,259), Spokane (177,196), Tacoma (176,664)
Statehood	November 11, 1889 Rank: 42nd
Principal rivers	Columbia, Snake, Spokane
Highest point	Mt. Rainier, 14,410 feet (4,395 m)
Motto	*Alki* (By and By)
Song	"Washington, My Home"

HALL OF MOSSES

In Olympic National Park, on the Olympic Peninsula, lush carpets of fern, mosses, and forest flowers line the rain-soaked forest. After California's Giant Redwood trees, this park's Sitka spruces and Douglas firs are the tallest trees in the United States — many as tall as a 25-story building. During the winter months the forests get as much as 140 inches (356 cm) of rain.

STATE SYMBOLS

Goldfinch

Western hemlock

MT. ST. HELENS

On May 18, 1980, Mt. St. Helens, in the Cascade Range, erupted with the force of an atomic bomb. The volcano had lain dormant for 123 years. It was the first volcanic eruption in the continental United States since 1917, and by far the most violent. Sixty people were killed by the eruption, and hundreds of miles of surrounding forests were covered with gray ash. The remains of Douglas firs burned and broken by the explosion's force have been left as "exhibits" at a special Volcanic Monument.

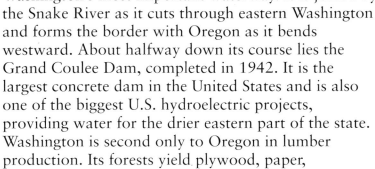

Coast rhododendron

THE APPLE STATE
Washington is the leading apple producer in the United States — especially of the Red and Golden Delicious varieties. The western part of the state has a mild and wet climate which is ideal for growing this fruit. Apples are grown in the Yakima area, especially in Wenatchee, where there is an annual Apple Blossom Festival.

SEATTLE
The largest city in Washington, Seattle is a major lumber port and scientific center. The 607-foot (185-m) Space Needle, shown here, is clearly seen by anyone approaching the city by boat on the Puget Sound. It was built for Century 21, the world fair held in Seattle in 1962. The city also boasts a monorail system and other reminders of the fair. These include the Pacific Science Center with its interesting architecture and exhibits, the Opera House, Art Pavilion, and award-winning International Fountain.

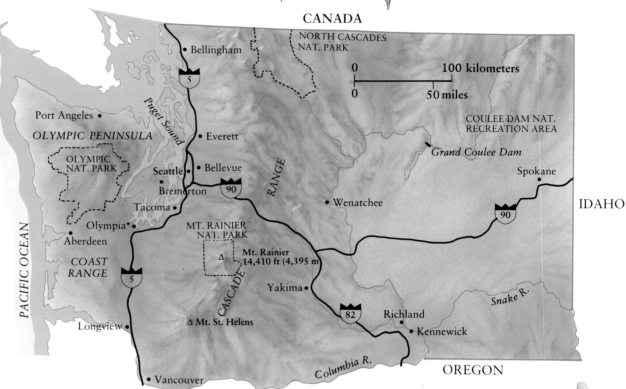

MULE DEER
The black-tailed, or mule, deer lives in the western United States, including Washington. Like other deer it feeds on leaves, fruit, grass, and sometimes moss, bark, and twigs — all of which exist in abundance in the western portion of the state. Speed is the deer's main defense against many predators — human and animal. This deer can reach speeds of 30 miles per hour (48 km/h).

WASHINGTON'S PORTS
Tacoma docks seen from an aerial view. Tacoma grew up around a sawmill and today is the center of a large forest-products industry. Several ports on Puget Sound have shipbuilding facilities, and there is an enormous amount of trade, both import and export, conducted through such ports as Tacoma and Seattle, with other Pacific Ocean ports, particularly in Asia. There is commercial fishing on Puget Sound.

BOEING JETS
The metropolitan area of Seattle is the location for several Boeing plants, which turn out aircraft and aerospace equipment. Aircraft manufacturing is a leading industry in Washington. The Boeing Corporation has been making aircraft and aircraft parts there since World War II, when it was the largest employer in the state. The business depends on orders from the U.S. Defense Department, and from air lines.

Boeing 747

Boeing KC-135 Stratotanker

WEST VIRGINIA

West Virginia was once part of Virginia. It became a state out of the turmoil of the Civil War. In 1861, Virginia voted to withdraw from the Union, but delegates from some of the western counties rebelled against this and set up their own "state" which they called Kanawha. During the war, in 1863, this temporary arrangement was officially accepted by Congress, and West Virginia became the 35th state of the Union.

To the north of West Virginia are Maryland and Pennsylvania, while the western border is with Ohio and Kentucky; Virginia lies to the east and south. West Virginia is nicknamed the "Mountain State" because it has the highest elevation east of the Mississippi River. Much of West Virginia's land is too rocky for cultivation. It is also fairly isolated from other states and commercial centers — cut off by the Appalachian Range, with its thickly wooded slopes, deep gorges, and valleys.

Because of this its people have been faced with many economic problems. After World War II, while the country as a whole enjoyed prosperity, West Virginia suffered a recession. Since the 1950s many West Virginians have left the state. For those who remain to work the land, the best farmland is in the Ohio and Kanawha river valleys. The latter is rich bluegrass country which supports livestock farming. Milk, eggs, and honey are also important farm products. The major West Virginia crops are apples and peaches. Manufacturing is important to the state's economy, especially chemical and metal products. Coal, natural gas, and oil mining are also major industries. The towns of Williamstown and Milton are famous glassmaking centers. Although heavily industrialized, West Virginia also has much unspoiled countryside. Tourism serves as another source of income for the state. Harpers Ferry is a famous historic site, and the mineral springs of White Sulphur Springs and Berkeley Springs have been attracting visitors for over 150 years.

Sugar maple

Cardinal

STATE SYMBOLS

Rhododendron

A MOUNTAINOUS STATE
The Appalachian Mountains, including the Blue Ridge range, form a high boundary between West Virginia and Virginia, and include the state's highest mountain, Spruce Knob. Virtually all of West Virginia is mountainous and the average elevation of the state is 1,500 feet (450 m). This region also includes most of the Potomac River Basin. The area is heavily forested, and the Monongahela National Forest alone covers 1,642,000 acres (665,000 hectares).

HARPERS FERRY
Standing where the Potomac meets the Shenandoah River, Harpers Ferry is an attractive, historic town, and site of the famous event in 1859 when anti-slavery campaigner John Brown seized the U.S. Arsenal in a violent attempt to free some slaves. The restored town includes forges, a tavern, a post office, and other buildings of the pre-Civil War years. John Brown was forced to surrender by Lieutenant Colonel Robert E. Lee, and was tried and convicted of treason against Virginia and hanged.

WEST VIRGINIA

Capital
Charleston
Area
24,232 sq. mi
(62,760 sq. km)
Population
1,793,477 (1990)
Largest cities
Charleston (57,287),
Huntington (54,844),
Wheeling (34,882)
Statehood
June 20, 1863
Rank: 35th
Principal rivers
Ohio, Potomac
Highest point
Spruce Knob,
4,861 feet (1,483 m)
Motto
Montani Semper Liberi
(Mountaineers Are
Always Free)
Song
"The West Virginia Hills"

CHARLESTON
Much of West Virginia's industry is centered around Charleston, the capital and largest city of the state. An impressive State Capitol faces the Kanawha River and also houses a natural history and art museum. Many consumer products such as nylon were developed in the area, and tourists can visit the chemical plants.

ANCIENT MOUNDS
One of the largest Native American burial mounds is the Grave Creek Mound in the appropriately named Moundsville. A museum contains relics that have been found there of a people dating from the first century B.C. Most of the large mounds were used for burial purposes. Statues such as this have helped archaeologists discover the age and purpose of these mounds.

COAL MINING
Coal seams run under half of West Virginia, making it the possessor of one of the richest coal deposits in the country. The state ranks as one of the top-three coal-producers in the U.S., along with neighboring Kentucky. Most of the biggest mines are in the southwestern part of the state where coal was first discovered in 1742. The coal-mining industry has experienced many bitter strikes, in which violence between miners and company guards has taken many lives. Because it is cheap, local coal is used to produce steam and electric power. Coal is also the source of chemicals used in the manufacture of records, cosmetics, and plastics.

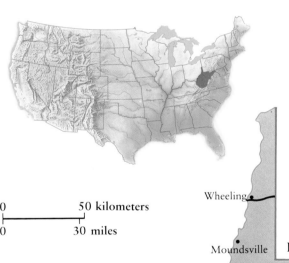

FINGER LAKE
One of the largest lakes in West Virginia, Sutton Lake is a typical finger lake — long and narrow — and lies near the center of the state. The state has many rivers, including the Ohio River, which forms West Virginia's western border, and the Potomac to the northeast.

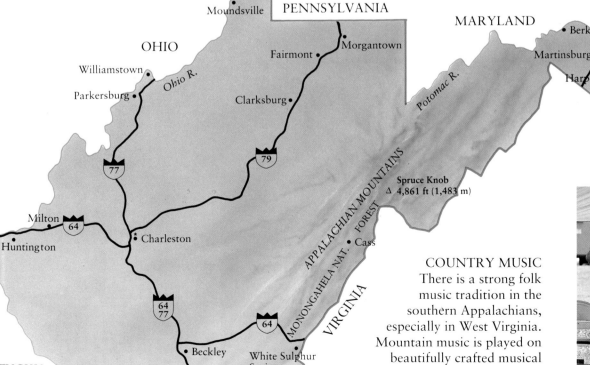

COUNTRY MUSIC
There is a strong folk music tradition in the southern Appalachians, especially in West Virginia. Mountain music is played on beautifully crafted musical instruments, such as fiddles, banjos, guitars, and dulcimers, accompanied by singing and dancing.

0 | 50 kilometers
0 | 30 miles

Wheeling

Moundsville

PENNSYLVANIA

MARYLAND

OHIO

Fairmont Morgantown

Berkeley Springs

Martinsburg

Williamstown

Ohio R.

Harpers Ferry

Parkersburg

Clarksburg

Potomac R.

79

APPALACHIAN MOUNTAINS

Spruce Knob
△ 4,861 ft (1,483 m)

77

Milton

64

Charleston

FOREST

Cass

Huntington

MONONGAHELA NAT.

VIRGINIA

64
77

64

KENTUCKY

Beckley White Sulphur Springs

77

Bluefield

WISCONSIN

The north Midwestern state of Wisconsin is almost completely surrounded by water. Lake Michigan lies to the east, the Menominee River to the northeast, Lake Superior forms the northern border, and the St. Croix and Mississippi rivers form the western border. Within the state there are more than 8,000 lakes. The low-lying, rolling plains with their lush pastures are ideal for dairy cattle, and Wisconsin produces much of the nation's milk, cheese, and butter. The state's many farms also grow fruit and vegetables, including corn, peas, tomatoes, cranberries, and cherries. Beef cattle and hogs are raised, especially in the south. Once a major lumber producer, Wisconsin has embarked on a program of forest conservation. Forests cover half the state, the most significant trees being ash, aspen, and elm. The lake port cities are key industrial centers, and fishing in the two Great Lakes is important to the state's industry. Water pollution, however, is a problem.

Wisconsin has hot summers and icy winters, though the weather on the lake shores is milder all year round. The state's main mineral resource is lead, which was mined quite early in its history. Stone is also quarried. Wisconsin's lake shores are much favored by travelers and tourists, as are the Chequamegon and Nicolet national forests. The latter is named after Jean Nicolet, a French explorer, who was the first to see the Wisconsin area in the 1600s. French fur traders, trappers, and missionaries followed, but the British took control in 1763 after the French and Indian War. Many settlers from the East and immigrants from Europe arrived between 1830 and 1850. Wisconsin joined the Union in 1848.

MILWAUKEE
The largest city in the state, Milwaukee is a busy commercial center in the Midwest. The city is home to many European immigrants, including Poles and Germans. When French fur trappers first arrived there in the 1600s, they heard local Native Americans referring to the place as *Mahn-a-waukee Seepe*, which means "Gathering Place by the River." Milwaukee stands on Lake Michigan, where the Milwaukee and Menomonee rivers meet. Its fine harbor is open most of the year and is accessible by the largest ships using the Great Lakes and the St. Lawrence Seaway.

DAIRY FARMING
After manufacturing, the most important business in Wisconsin is farming. Of the 80,000 farms, over half are geared to dairying, and the state is known as "America's Dairyland." Each October, in Madison, the state capital, there is a World Dairy Expo, which features Wisconsin's dairy animals and products. Turkeys, pigs, chickens, and sheep are also raised. Corn, beans, peas, hay, oats, and cabbage are grown.

WISCONSIN

Capital
Madison
Area
56,153 sq. mi
(145,436 sq. km)
Population
4,891,769 (1990)
Largest cities
Milwaukee (628,088),
Madison (191,262),
Green Bay (96,466)
Statehood
May 29, 1848
Rank: 30th
Principal rivers
Wisconsin,
Mississippi, Chippewa
Highest point
Timms Hill,
1,951 feet (595 m)
Motto
Forward
Song
"On, Wisconsin!"

STATE SYMBOLS

Robin

Sugar maple

Wood violet

ORSON WELLES
Born in Wisconsin on May 6, 1915, actor, director, producer, and writer Orson Welles was one of the most influential Americans in the motion picture industry. His film *Citizen Kane* (1941), based on the life of a newspaper tycoon, is considered one of the finest films ever made.

BREWERY
Milwaukee is famous as a beer-producing city. Its beers are canned, bottled, and shipped all over the world. Brewing was started by German immigrants in the 1840s. This is Pabst Brewery, which produces one of the best-known beers in the world. Visitors may tour one of the city's breweries.

BADGERS
Wisconsin is nicknamed the "Badger State" after these distinctive black and white striped members of the weasel family. They are found mainly in the central plains from southern Canada down to Mexico. They use the long, heavy, blunt claws on their front feet for digging burrows, or dens.

WISCONSIN DELLS
The Wisconsin River winds through the Wisconsin Dells — scenic gorges carved by the river's strong currents. The channel is up to 150 feet (45 m) deep. The river starts near the Wisconsin-Michigan border and flows through the center of the state past rapids and the Dells. Tourism is important in this area. The Wisconsin eventually joins the Mississippi River after a course of 430 miles (690 km). The river is navigable by small craft for about half its length.

117

WYOMING

A land of wide, open spaces, Wyoming ranks in the top-ten states for size, but has the smallest population. The state is known for its beautiful mountain scenery and for being the site of the country's oldest national park — Yellowstone. Over half of Wyoming's land, including Yellowstone, is owned by the U.S. government, which controls grazing and logging.

The state is a near-perfect rectangle in shape, stretching 367 miles (591 km) from east to west, and 278 miles (448 km) from north to south. There are two main types of terrain: high plains and mountains. This gives Wyoming the second highest overall elevation, after Colorado. Even the lowest point is 3,100 feet (945 m) above sea level. The mainly arid soil is not particularly fertile and much of the state's income is derived from oil and oil refining. Cattle ranching is also important and Wyoming has ten times as many cattle as people.

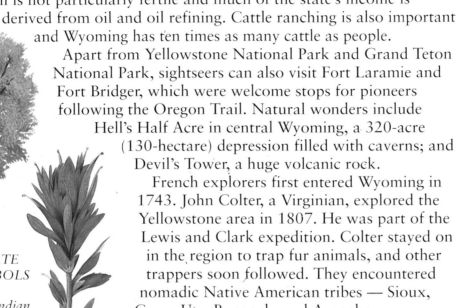

Cottonwood

STATE SYMBOLS

Western meadowlark

Indian paintbrush

Apart from Yellowstone National Park and Grand Teton National Park, sightseers can also visit Fort Laramie and Fort Bridger, which were welcome stops for pioneers following the Oregon Trail. Natural wonders include Hell's Half Acre in central Wyoming, a 320-acre (130-hectare) depression filled with caverns; and Devil's Tower, a huge volcanic rock.

French explorers first entered Wyoming in 1743. John Colter, a Virginian, explored the Yellowstone area in 1807. He was part of the Lewis and Clark expedition. Colter stayed on in the region to trap fur animals, and other trappers soon followed. They encountered nomadic Native American tribes — Sioux, Crow, Ute, Bannock, and Arapaho.

As Wyoming was first to grant women the vote, in 1869, it is called the Equality State.

WYOMING	
Capital	
Cheyenne	
Area	
97,809 sq. mi	
(253,325 sq. km)	
Population	
453,588 (1990)	
Largest cities	
Cheyenne (50,008),	
Casper (46,742),	
Laramie (26,687)	
Statehood	
July 10, 1890	
Rank: 44th	
Principal rivers	
Bighorn, Green,	
North Platte	
Highest point	
Gannett Peak,	
13,785 feet (4,202 m)	
Motto	
Equal Rights	
Song	
"Wyoming"	

YELLOWSTONE NATIONAL PARK

In the northwest corner of Wyoming lie 3,472 square miles (8,992 sq. km) of Yellowstone National Park which spreads into Montana and Idaho. The park was established in 1872, the first of its kind in the world. Within the park are some 10,000 geysers, hot springs, mud volcanoes, fossil forests, and several canyons and waterfalls, as well as the 1,000-foot (305-m) deep canyon and 308-foot (94-m) high waterfall of the Yellowstone River. A wide variety of animals, including bison, moose, elk, deer, and bighorn sheep, roam freely here in their natural habitat. The park attracts some 2 million visitors each year, creating problems for the ecological balance of the area.

Morning Glory Pool, pictured here, is a hydrothermal pool — one with steam-heated water. Several kinds of algae of different colors grow in water at different temperature levels. The waters are crystal clear, fading into deep aquamarine. Animals are drawn to such thermal pools.

CATTLE RANCHERS

A young rancher tries his skill at rounding up cattle. Because the soil is so arid and grass so scarce, it takes as many as 50 acres (20 hectares) to feed one cow. Cowboys also perform in the state rodeos. Some work on dude ranches, resorts that offer tourists a flavor of ranch life.

DEVIL'S TOWER

In northeastern Wyoming stands the impressive Devil's Tower. It was formed by the upsurge of molten lava millions of years ago in the Black Hills. Designated the country's first national monument in 1906, it is a vertical mass of volcanic rock, rising 865 feet (264 m) from its base. Many moviegoers will recognize it as inspiring the scene for the spaceship landing in Steven Spielberg's classic science fiction film *Close Encounters of the Third Kind* (1977).

ELK HERDS

North of Jackson Hole is the National Elk Refuge with a herd of 7,500 elk. The elk gather there in winter for feeding, pawing through the snow to reach the dense grasses on the plains. Visitors can take a supervised sleigh ride through the herd.

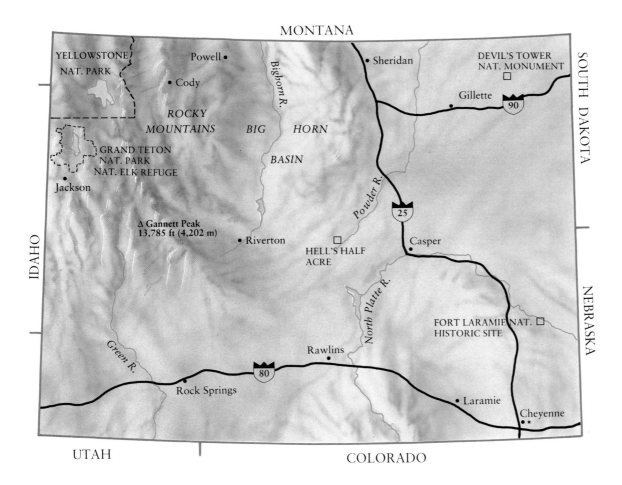

OIL DRILLING

Wyoming ranks tenth in the United States in mineral production. The chief industry is oil refining. Here, oil workers use the heavy drills to extract more of this precious commodity. Wyoming has vast reserves of other energy-producing minerals. Because it is also a major producer of hydroelectric power, it exports power to other states.

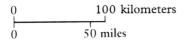

NELLIE TAYLOE ROSS

The first woman governor in the United States was Nellie Tayloe Ross. She was elected to succeed her late husband as governor of Wyoming in 1924, 16 days before another woman governor was elected in Texas. She was later appointed director of the U.S. Mint — making her one of the first women in the United States to also hold such an important federal post.

OUTLYING U.S. AREAS

Apart from the 50 states and the District of Columbia, which make up the United States, there is one Caribbean commonwealth and a number of Pacific islands and atolls under U.S. trusteeship. This means that they come under U.S. protection and receive U.S. financial and military assistance. More importantly for the islanders, it means they are all U.S. citizens, although they cannot vote in U.S. presidential elections when living in the territories. Of these outlying U.S. areas the single largest and most important is the Commonwealth of Puerto Rico. It consists of beautiful islands lying between the Atlantic Ocean to the north and the Caribbean Sea to the south, 1,040 miles (1,673 km) southwest of Miami, Florida. Each year about 1.5 million tourists enjoy Puerto Rico's sandy beaches and pleasant mild climate, with a mean temperature of 77° F (25° C), and tourism earns the island over $1 billion each year.

Christopher Columbus landed on the island in 1493, at a time when the Arawak people inhabited the land. It is believed to be the only part of the United States where Columbus ever set foot. The U.S. took control of the island from Spain, following the Spanish-American War of 1898, and it became a commonwealth in 1952. Most of the residents still speak Spanish as their first language.

PUERTO RICO

Capital
San Juan
Area
3,435 sq. mi
(8,897 sq. km)
Population
3,336,000 (1990)
Principal river
Arecibo
Highest point
Cerro de Punta,
4,390 feet (1,339 m)
Motto
*Joannes Est Nomen
Eius* (John Is His Name)
Song (national anthem)
"*La Borinqueña*"

The second-largest U.S. territory after Puerto Rico is Guam, one of the Mariana Islands. The Mariana, Marshall, and Caroline archipelagos (groups of small islands) form what is called the Trust Territory of the Pacific Islands. The U.S. is responsible to the United Nations for their political and economic well-being.

BANANAS

About 70 percent of Puerto Rico's land is farmland, and bananas are the major fruit crop. Bananas and plantains, which are starchy fruits similar to bananas, are grown inland in most regions of the island. Exotic fruits such as papayas and star apples are also cultivated.

PUERTO RICO

The first Spanish settlement on the island was built in 1509 following the conquest of the island by the Spanish explorer Ponce de León. It was situated at Caparra, across the bay from the capital, San Juan, pictured here. The island's income used to come from trade in slaves, gold, and sugar cane.

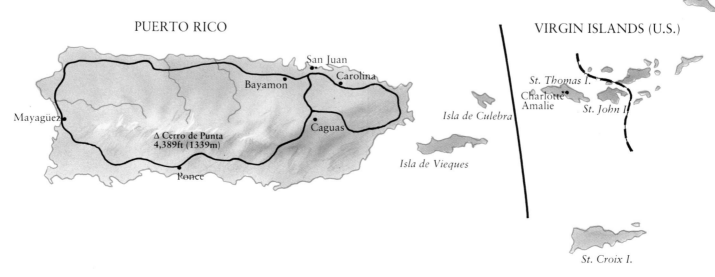

PUERTO RICO

San Juan
Carolina
Bayamon
Mayagüez
△ Cerro de Punta
4,389ft (1339m)
Caguas
Ponce

VIRGIN ISLANDS (U.S.)

St. Thomas I.
Charlotte
Amalie
St. John I.
Isla de Culebra
Isla de Vieques
St. Croix I.

GUAM
The largest and southernmost of the Mariana Islands, Guam, is a U.S. territory. It is known as the place "Where America's day begins" because it lies west of the International Date Line. Guam is 209 square miles (541 sq. km) in size. It has a large U.S. air base which was important during the Vietnam War.

DUGOUT CANOES
Ocean-going dugout canoes with outriggers ply the Pacific islands. Many, such as these, are converted for sailing, with a single canvas sail. Some fishing is done from these canoes.

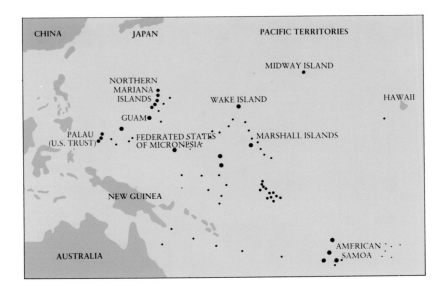

SAMOAN HOUSE
American Samoans make their stilted houses from the local materials on the islands, such as coconut tree trunks and fronds. The people are of Polynesian origin, like those of Hawaii, and work and live in family and village groups. American Samoa is made up of six islands and is the most southerly of all lands under U.S. sovereignty. Most inhabitants live in and around Pago Pago on Tutuila Island.

VIRGIN ISLANDS
Charlotte Amalie is the capital of the American Virgin Islands, which consist of St. Thomas, St. John, and St. Croix. The islands lie 70 miles (113 km) east of Puerto Rico. Charlotte Amalie, on St. Thomas, is a major port. Its main industries include tourism, rum, textiles, perfumes, and watches.

COFFEE BEANS
Coffee competes with sugar cane as the most valuable crop of Puerto Rico. It is grown in the western part of the central mountains. The picture shows a coffee plant with clusters of ripening fruit. The fruit is red and is called a cherry. Each cherry contains two beans which are roasted, ground, and sold for making into the drink called coffee.

CARNIVAL
The original Spanish influence still pervades many of Puerto Rico's festivals and celebrations. Each town has a patron saint, and saints' days are celebrated with music festivals and carnivals such as this. The largest festival is in San Juan, in summer. It was once directed by the island's most famous resident, the cellist Pablo Casals.

FACTS AND FIGURES

MT. McKINLEY
The highest mountain in the United States is Mt. McKinley in Alaska.

REDWOOD TREES
The tallest trees in the United States are the giant redwoods of California.

FAULT LINE
The San Andreas fault stretches 750 miles (1,200 km) north to south in California.

UNITED STATES FACTS
Total Area of the United States 3,618,770 sq. miles (9,371,900 sq. km)

Widest point
From coast to coast (excluding Hawaii and Alaska) the United States measures 2,807 miles (4,519 km)

Highest point
Mt. McKinley, Alaska 20,320 feet (6,194 m)

Lowest point
Death Valley, California, 282 feet (86 m) below sea level

Highest state
Colorado, average mean elevation, 6,800 feet (2,070 m)

Lowest state
Delaware, average mean elevation, 60 feet (18 m)

Northernmost point
Point Barrow, Alaska

Southernmost point
South Cape, Hawaii

Easternmost point
West Quoddy Head, Maine

Westernmost point
Cape Wrangell, Alaska

Largest lakes
Superior, 31,820 sq. miles (82,414 sq. km)
Huron, 23,010 sq. miles (59,596 sq. km)
Michigan, 22,400 sq. miles (88,016 sq. km)

Longest rivers
Mississippi, 2,340 miles (3,766 km)
Missouri, 2,315 miles (3,725 km)
Rio Grande, 1,760 miles (2,8320 km)
Arkansas, 1,459 miles (2,348 km)
Colorado, 1,450 miles (2,333 km)

Coastline
The United States has 12,383 miles (19,937 km) of coastline

Geographic center
48 states: near Lebanon, Kansas; all 50 states: Butte County, South Dakota

Highest human settlement
Climax, Colorado, 11,560 feet (3,526 m), well over 2 miles (3 km) high

Lowest human settlement
Calipatria, California, 185 feet (56 m) below sea level

Largest national park
Wrangell-St. Elias, Alaska, 13,018 sq. miles (33,717 sq. km)

Tallest structure
A TV tower in Blanchard, North Dakota, 2,063 feet (629 m) high

Highest bridge
Royal Gorge, in Colorado, 1,053 feet (321 m) above water

Tallest building
Sears Tower, Chicago, Illinois, 1,454 feet (443 m) high

KODIAK BEAR
The largest bear in the United States, and the world, is the Kodiak bear from Alaska.

L.A. SMOG
The worst air pollution in the United States occurs in the Greater Los Angeles area.

CALIFORNIA CONDOR
The California condor is virtually extinct. As of mid-1990 there were only about 40 birds left.

MAP INDEX

GENERAL INDEX

PHOTOGRAPHIC ACKNOWLEDGEMENTS

The publishers wish to thank Zefa for supplying most of the photographs inside this book. Additional photographs were supplied by:

Allsport: p.53 top; Paul Bahn: p.101 center left; Gary A.M. Browne: p.22 bottom; J. Allan Cash: p.8 bottom, p.13 top right, p.21 bottom right, p.26 bottom, p.43 top, p.60 left, p.65 bottom, p.67 top, p.73 top left, p.98 top, p.108 top, p.111 top; Bruce Coleman Ltd: p.12 top, p.42 top, p.119 top, p.120 right, p.121 top right and center left; Colorsport: p.47 top, p.88 left; Dermot Curnyn: p.31 top left; Delaware state travel and tourism dept.: p.35 center; Michael Dent: p.114 center left; Lawrence Englesberg: p.11 center; Mary Evans Picture Library: p.33 bottom center, p.57 bottom right; Eye Ubiquitous: p.76 bottom right, p.105 top; Ronald Grant Archive: p.117 top; Susan Griggs Agency: p.7 top and bottom, p.8 top, p.10 bottom, p.49 top, p.51 center left and bottom left, p.53 center and center right, p.55 bottom, p.65 top and center, p.71 bottom, p.78 top, p.79 top left, p.95 top right, p.109 center, p.115 top right, p.118 bottom right; Robert Harding Picture Library: p.14 top, p.15 bottom, p.29 center left, p.31 center right, p.38 bottom right, p.39 bottom left, p.52 bottom, p.56 bottom left, p.66 top, p.75 center left, p.77 bottom, p.80 top and bottom, p.89 center, p.96 bottom, p.97 center, p.107 bottom, p.110 bottom left and bottom right, p.111 bottom, p.121 top left; Grant Heilman: p.27 top left, p.30 bottom, p.35 top, p.39 bottom right, p.43 bottom, p.48 bottom, p.67 bottom, p.73 top right, p.75 bottom, p.90 top, p.116 bottom; Hulton Picture Company: p.20 bottom left, p.21 bottom left, p.27 top right, p.28 right, p.40 right, p.51 center right, p.58 center, p.62 center, p.68 left, p.89 center right, p.90 bottom right, p.100 center, p.119 bottom center; The Hutchison Library: p.33 bottom, p.91 center, p.115 bottom; The Image Bank: p.17 top left, p.56 bottom right, p.69 bottom; Kos Photos/ Sharon Green: p.97 top; Magnum: p.89 bottom right (Erich Hartman); NAACP: p.39 center; New Jersey Dept. of Travel and Tourism: p.78 bottom left; Peter Newark Pictures: p.54 bottom, p.59 top center, p.66 bottom, p.91 bottom; Photo Researchers Inc.: p.53 bottom left, p.115 top right; Popperfoto: p.45 bottom; Science Photo Library: p. 99 top; Sefton Photo Library: p.55 top; Phil Sheldon Golf Picture Library: p.99 right; Stockmarket: p.20 bottom, p.93 top; Tony Stone Worldwide: p.17 bottom left, p.21 top, p.23 top right, p.26 top, p.27 center, p.35 bottom, p.44 bottom, p.57 top, p.58 bottom center, p.62 bottom, p.68 right, p.72 top, p.77 top, p.85 top, p.96 top, p.100 top, p.108 bottom, p.109 bottom, p.116 top, p.117 center and bottom, p.121 bottom right; TRIP: p.83 top (R. Fairer-Smith); Valan Photos: p.79 top right; West Virginia Government Office: p.115 center; Wichita Art Museum: p.95 bottom left.